WHEN I SEE THE BLOOD

JIMMY SWAGGART

JIMMY SWAGGART MINISTRIES
P.O. Box 262550 | Baton Rouge, Louisiana 70826-2550
www.jsm.org

ISBN 978-1-941403-26-6

09-132 | COPYRIGHT © 2016 Jimmy Swaggart Ministries®

16 17 18 19 20 21 22 23 24 25 / EBM / 10 9 8 7 6 5 4 3 2 1

TABLE OF CONTENTS

INTRODUCTION

INTRODUCTION

UNDER THE INSPIRATION OF the Holy Spirit, Simon Peter stated: *"Forasmuch as you know that you were not redeemed with corruptible things, as silver and gold ... But with the precious blood of Christ, as of a lamb without blemish and without spot"* (I Pet. 1:18-19).

WHY BLOOD?

The Scripture says, *"The life of the flesh is in the blood"* (Lev. 17:11).

I think one can say without fear of contradiction that Chapter 12 of Exodus gives us an account in shadow and in type of the worth of the precious blood of Christ, which alone can bring about deliverance.

The mighty miracles performed by Moses in Egypt failed to move Pharaoh. However, the shed blood of the lamb, which was a type of Christ—and especially the blood applied to the doorposts—brought about Israel's total and complete deliverance. It must be understood that God did not look so much at who was in the house but whether the blood was applied to the doorposts of the house.

With the latter being accomplished, it meant that for those in the house, whomever they may have been—whether spiritually weak or spiritually strong—all were safe. It has not changed from then until now.

We are saved not because of inherent goodness, of which we have none. We are saved because our faith and our trust is in Christ and what He did for us at Calvary's Cross in the shedding of His life's blood, which effected salvation for all who will believe. Salvation is so simple! In fact, it is so easy that all you have to do is just simply believe, and do so with all of your heart. Then, instantly, every sin is washed away by the precious shed blood of the Lord Jesus Christ.

REDEMPTION

The Holy Spirit through the apostle plainly told us that we were not redeemed with corruptible things such as silver and gold. Redemption presents a work that was accomplished by Christ Jesus on Calvary and is, therefore, so far as we are concerned, entirely objective. We could have no part in it, for we committed the sins that made it necessary. If not for what Christ did at Calvary, we would have been left to die in our iniquities. God forbid!

This means that salvation is all of God and none at all of us. The truth is, Jesus died on the Cross, whether sinful man liked it or not. However, when it comes to regeneration or the new birth, that is subjective. In other words, we play a part in this in that we have to evidence faith in what Christ has already done, which means that we are yielding to the Holy Spirit.

It is easy to fall into the habit of preaching about the gospel but not actually preaching the gospel itself; however, when we speak on and expound a text like this, we are brought back to the heart of the gospel message of Christ. This is one way of discovering whether the message is of God or of men.

THE CROSS

If the message is about the Cross, which means that, in some way, it streams toward the Cross or proceeds from the Cross, then it's of God. Otherwise, it's of men!

If we properly understand the Cross, then we understand that the entirety of the Bible is, in effect, the story of the Cross because the Bible is the story of the redemption of man, and man was redeemed by the price that Jesus paid at the Cross.

Redemption here means that we were rescued from sin and death by the blood of Christ as the valuable consideration on account of which it was done. That is, the blood or the life of Christ offered as a sacrifice effected the same purpose in regard to justice and to the maintenance of the principles of moral government, which the punishment of the sinner himself would have done.

To say it another way, it was that which God was pleased to accept in the place of the punishment of the sinner as answering to the same great ends in His administration. The principles of His truth and justice could be maintained in this way the same as if it were the punishment of the guilty themselves. If this is true, then there is no obstacle to our salvation, and on repentance and faith in what Christ has done for us, we might be consistently pardoned.

SILVER AND GOLD

The highest form of exchange in the commerce of men is silver and gold, or that which relates to these precious metals. When Peter wrote these words, at least a third of the Roman Empire consisted of slaves. These slaves were bought with silver and gold or sold for silver and gold. So, when Peter made this statement, his words would have had an even greater meaning in his day than they do presently. It was common in those days to see slaves auctioned off to the highest bidder. Silver and gold would change hands, and the individual would then belong to a new master.

Sometime back, Frances and I were with friends in New Orleans, Louisiana. We were standing on a street corner waiting for a restaurant to open. I looked to my right and spotted one of the historical markers that are quite common in certain parts of our nation.

This marker, however, somewhat startled me because it spoke of the fact that on that particular corner, the slave market of New Orleans once stood.

It was there that Abraham Lincoln, the Illinois rail-splitter, stood and watched the proceedings—proceedings, incidentally, of extreme cruelty—and vowed in his heart, "God, if You will give me the ability, I will smite this curse of slavery that plagues this land."

God took this man at his word and made him the president of the United States. A bloody civil war was fought, and many men died, but Lincoln stood true to his word. During his time in office, Congress produced the Emancipation Proclamation, which, in effect, outlawed the terrible scourge of slavery in America.

SLAVERY

The sad fact is, there is a far worse slavery that is incumbent upon all men than even the slavery that I have just mentioned. It is the slavery of sin, which gives Satan the right to hold men in bondage.

In the United States alone, it is said that there are 20 million alcoholics. As well, it is said that there are approximately 20 million men and women addicted to gambling. There are about 25 million drug addicts in this nation. But yet, every human being who doesn't know Christ is a slave to their passions in some way, whether these are mentioned or not.

Of course, unredeemed man bristles at the idea that he is a slave. In fact, he claims in the loudest voice possible that he is his own man, free to do what he likes. In reality, he is free to do what Satan likes and no more!

As a result of the fall, man is born in original sin, which, in effect, means that he is born a slave—a slave to passion and pride. We do have a problem!

Even though lost and, therefore, in slavery, the soul of each one of these individuals, whomever and wherever they might be, is of such value as to defy all description. In fact, it is so valuable that Jesus said: *"For what is a man profited, if he shall gain the whole world, and lose his own soul? or what shall a man give in exchange for his soul?"* (Mat. 16:26).

Because of this great worth, there is nothing on earth that can redeem a lost soul. So, if man, God's highest creation, is to be redeemed, God will have to perform the task from the worth of His own self. It will have to be a worth of far greater value than silver and gold. What could that be?

JESUS CHRIST

God became man, i.e., "the Lord Jesus Christ." He did so for many reasons, but the main reason of all was that He might pay the price for dying humanity. It was a price that He alone could pay, the payment of which would be His own life. God is Spirit, and He cannot die; therefore, in order for Him to die, He would have to become man.

The price that was demanded was high, in fact, higher than we could ever begin to comprehend; however, inasmuch as God paid the price Himself, man is left with no quarrel or argument.

So, to meet this need, Jesus Christ died as a sacrifice for sin. Let the reader understand that this was the reason He came, the reason He lived, and the reason He died.

It was for sin.

This is the only satisfactory account that can be given of that most wonderful of all events—the violent, shameful, painful, and accursed death of the innocent, the perfect, incarnate, only-begotten of God. This event would have been utterly inexplicable had we not been informed in a plain, well-accredited, divine revelation that this immaculately holy, this absolutely perfect, and this infinitely dignified person occupied the place of guilty men. This was by divine appointment to gain the most important and otherwise unattainable objects in the moral government of the universe. In occupying our place, He met with our desert, did what we were bound to do, suffered what we deserved to suffer, and did and suffered all that was necessary. In the estimation of infinite wisdom and righteousness, He lay a foundation for our pardon and salvation.

ISAIAH AND PAUL

"All we like sheep have gone astray; we have turned every one to his own way; and the Lord *has laid on Him (as the destined victim) the iniquity of us all"* (Isa. 53:6). The consequence was that exaction was made, and He became answerable. It pleased the Lord to bruise Him instead of destroying us, and *"He was wounded for our transgressions, He was bruised for our iniquities: the chastisement of our peace was upon Him; and with His stripes we are healed"* (Isa. 53:5). He *"bear our sins in His own body on the tree"* (I Pet. 2:24). He was made sin in our stead and died as the

Just One in the stead of the unjust. *He redeemed us from the curse of the broken law by becoming a curse in our stead* (Gal. 3:13).

The direct and primary end of this sacrifice, so far as man is concerned, was to effect a change in his relation to God, to lay a foundation for an alteration in our state, and to secure pardon and restoration to the enjoyment of the divine favor. However, the ultimate and most important end of this sacrifice in reference to man was, through this change of relation, to effect a change of disposition, and through this alteration of state, to secure a transformation of character.

RELIGION

The phrase, *"From your vain conversation* (lifestyle) *received by tradition from your fathers"* (I Pet. 1:18) proclaims the vast difference by comparison to what we have received from our heavenly Father.

Even though Peter was speaking directly of the Mosaic law, still, the word *fathers* refers also to the whole of humanity and that all babies are born in the likeness of Adam, which speaks of total depravity as a result of the fall.

When the blood of Christ was shed as a victim for sin, it was to deliver men from this vain lifestyle, which was the best that our earthly fathers could do. Even the great law of God that was given to Moses, which, of course, was perfect in every respect, was taken by man and twisted and perverted until it was hardly recognizable when Jesus came. It had succumbed to the place of mere tradition.

Deliverance from depravity is an essential part (the most important part in some points of view) of the Christian salvation. Deliverance from guilt and that sacrifice—which was sufficient to secure deliverance from guilt and is the grand means of securing this deliverance from depravity—were necessary.

THE ATONEMENT

As well, the connection of the atonement with sanctification, which we've been dealing with again and again, is frequently stated in Scripture and is one of the most peculiar and important principles of the Christian faith. Christ *"gave Himself for us, that He might redeem us from all iniquity, and purify unto Himself a peculiar people, zealous of good works"* (Titus 2:14).

Christ gave Himself for us *"that He might deliver* (redeem) *us from this present evil world"* (Gal. 1:4).

Christ sanctified Himself and devoted Himself to suffer as a sacrificial victim so that His people might be *"sanctified through the truth"* (Jn. 17:19). When He died for all, all died in Him; and He died for them, that they might not live to themselves, but to Him who died and rose again (II Cor. 5:14-15). *"Christ has redeemed us from the curse of the law, being made a curse for us* (in our place)," not only *"that the blessing of Abraham"* (a full and free justification) *"might come on the Gentiles* (us)," but *"that we* (also) *might receive* (obtain) *the promise of the Spirit,"* the source of all true holiness, *"through faith"* (by believing) (Gal. 3:13-14).

THE PRECIOUS BLOOD OF CHRIST

The phrase used by Simon Peter, *"But with the precious blood of Christ,"* presents the payment, which proclaims the poured out life of Christ on behalf of sinners.

The manner in which the shedding of the blood of Jesus Christ as the great sacrificial victim, which secures the holiness of all who believe in Him, may be stated in a few words. However, to fully and satisfactorily illustrate it would require more space than we can here devote to it.

By making the atonement consistent with the divine justice to confer spiritual blessings on sinners, it removes obstacles out of the way of their sanctification that would otherwise be insurmountable. By procuring for the Saviour (as one part of the reward of His generous labors and the cause of God's glory) the power of dispensing divine influence, it secures what is at once absolutely necessary and completely sufficient for making men holy. Finally, the statement of the truth about Christ, the Son of God, suffering and dying in the place of sinners (which is contained in the Scriptures) must be understood and believed. It is under divine influence and is the grand means of destroying that enmity against God that is in the sinner's mind. This is the elementary principle of all depravity and the kindling up in his heart the love of God.

This is the elementary principle of all holiness—of delivering the man from the demoralizing influence of the present evil world of things seen and temporal—and bringing him under the sanctifying influence of things unseen and eternal.

This, then, is the meaning of the apostle's statement in I Peter 1:18-19: "The blood of Christ has been shed to redeem you from your vain lifestyle, received by tradition from your fathers. The Son of God has died as a sacrifice for sin in order to secure your holiness."

THE CHRISTIAN AND REDEMPTION

Surely it does not require many words to show what Christ has done for us to provide an all-powerful motive for us to place our faith totally in His great finished work. This is true especially when we consider the price that He has paid for us. Has deliverance from depravity been secured at such a cost, and shall I pour contempt upon the divine generosity by looking elsewhere as it regards sanctification? Shall I counteract the great design of the death of Christ?

Though He shed His blood that I might be redeemed from my former vain lifestyle, shall I still fashion myself according to my former lusts in my ignorance? Shall I still hug the chains to break asunder, for which the Lord of glory toiled, bled, and died? Considering this, how can I, in whose place Christ died for sin, live any longer in sin? Reckoning myself as if I believe the truth, I well may—to have died to sin in Christ Jesus and to be alive in Christ Jesus to God (Rom.

6:11). Surely it is the most unnatural and incongruous of all things in me to allow sin (the sin nature) to reign in my mortal body, so that I should obey it by its desires (Rom. 6:12). Of course, I should not yield my members to sin as instruments of unrighteousness, but I should yield myself to God as one alive from the dead and my members to Him as instruments of righteousness (Rom. 6:12-14).

THE ONLY ANSWER FOR SIN

This, the sacrifice of Christ, is the answer for all the enticements of sin in the world, in fact, the only answer. Except you can offer my soul something beyond the price that was given for it on the Cross, I cannot hearken to you. Far be it from me that I should prefer a base lust—or anything in this world or it all—to Him who gave Himself to death for me and paid my ransom with His blood. His matchless love has freed me from the miserable captivity of sin and has forever fastened me to the sweet yoke of obedience. Let Him alone dwell and rule in me and let Him never go forth from my heart, who, for my sake, refused to come down from the Cross (Brown) .

BLOOD IN THE EYES OF GOD

In Genesis, Chapter 9, God says that man is not to eat flesh with blood in it because life is in the blood. Blood is precious to God; it is given on the altar as an atonement for our souls. In the Mosaic legislation, the people were prohibited from eating things strangled because the blood was still in the flesh.

The blood was used upon the altar and poured out at the base of the altar for an atonement for sin. The life of the flesh, as stated, is in the blood, and *"I have given it to you upon the altar to make an atonement for your souls: for it is the blood that makes an atonement for the soul"* (Lev. 17:11).

When the Lord looked upon the crimson of life poured out, even though it was that of a bullock or of a lamb, in God's sight, it was precious because it was a symbol of the blood that would be shed by His only Son.

The blood of a man is even more precious in His sight than that of an animal, as would be obvious. In Genesis, Chapter 9, God says that if a man's life is taken in cold blood, the person who took his life must pay for it with his own blood (Gen. 9:6). In the book of Numbers, God says the shedding of blood by violence (by murder) defiles the land (Num. 35:33). It cries to God as the blood of Abel cried to the Lord of heaven (Gen. 4:10).

THE BLOOD OF GOD'S ONLY SON

If the blood of animals and the blood of men are precious to God, what shall we say about the blood of God's Son, our redeeming Saviour? In Acts 20:28, the Apostle Paul says that the church was purchased by the blood of Christ. This is an amazing and astonishing expression. In fact, everything about the atonement is beyond comprehension. If there is anything that defies description, it is the atoning death of Christ. How does the blood wash away our sins? What are the sufferings of Christ into which we can hardly enter?

To be frank, we can but little enter into the mysteries of the atoning grace of God and Jesus Christ. The first thing we must know is that the blood of Christ brings to us God's atoning grace. The law says, *"This do and you shall live."* We are to obey this commandment, and we will have eternal life. How does a man keep the law of God, and how can he learn to be perfect in all his ways when his every effort is characterized by mistake and sin?

WHAT DOES THE BLOOD OF CHRIST DO FOR US?

So, the man under the old economy of God brought for his sin a sacrifice. He came before God with a bullock or a lamb but had to come again and again. So, his life was one of perpetual memory of his sin and shortcomings.

Likewise, the high priest went into the Holy of Holies with the blood of expatiation, and he returned again. In fact, it had to be done every year. There was no end. However, what does the blood of Christ do for us?

Paul writes in Romans 10:4: *"For Christ is the end of the law for righteousness to everyone who believes."* In Romans 5:9, he tells us that we are now *"justified by His blood,"* and *"we shall be saved from wrath through Him."*

Christ is the end of the law, which means that He has satisfied the demands of the broken law in every capacity.

If we look in faith to Him, His blood will redeem us from the wrath and judgment of God upon our sins. Outside of Christ, we are slaves to the tyrant of the law. The law threatens us, curses us, and judges us. There is no righteous man before the law. All have sinned and come short of the expectation of God. What does a man do, therefore, who finds himself always a sinner? The blood of Christ brings to him the grace of God. Under the shelter of God's love, mercy, and grace, the judgments have been placated.

THE BLOOD OF CHRIST AND
THE WASHING OF SINS

It is through the blood of Christ, and the blood of Christ only, that our sins are washed away. We are not saved by His miraculous birth, even though that was necessary, or by His beautiful life, although that was necessary. We were not saved by His miracles that could even change the course of nature, even though those were necessary. It was not even by His words of wisdom, though never a man spoke like this man, and that was necessary. We are saved solely by the blood of the Cross, and it is that which we must never forget.

As well, the death of Christ is not an exemplar. In other words, He did not die to teach us an example. He did not die for our inspiration, but according to the Scriptures, He died for our sins. What God seeks in us is a response of humility, repentance, and acceptance so that through the blood of the Son of God, we might be cleansed, and we might be acceptable in His sight. This is no accident in history, and neither is it something that just sort of happened as it regarded the plan of God.

The apostle said that the spilling of the precious blood of Christ was foreordained before the foundation of the world, before God flung the stars and the planets into space, and before He created this earth.

Christ died for our sins according to the foreknowledge and sovereign elective grace of God. It was in the blood of Christ that the church was born. It is in the blood of Christ that we are justified. It is in the blood of Christ that we have hope of forgiveness for sins, and by the blood of Christ, He has quenched all the altar fires on the earth.

THE ALTAR FIRES HAVE BEEN QUENCHED

It is difficult for us in this modern day to realize that in the day of the Egyptian, the Babylonian, the Assyrian, the Greek, and the Roman, the entire earth was covered with altars and the smoke of fires ascending up to heaven.

As far as I know, there is not one altar burning in the earth today. Why?

The atoning grace of God in Christ Jesus quenched all the altar fires on the earth. There are no more priestly orders, for He is our High Priest, making intercession for us in the sanctuary of God.

Our Lord was obedient to the law for us in His life. In death, He paid the penalty of sin for us. In His death, He was the scapegoat that carried away the sins of His people. In the resurrection, He not only was declared to be the Son of God, but He also brought justification to declare us righteous in His presence when He comes again. In His return, He will bring to us a complete salvation.

It will be the completed redemption of the purchased possession, a resurrected, immortalized body, as well as a redeemed and blood-bought soul.

THE BLOOD OF CHRIST AND REGENERATION

What has the blood of Jesus Christ done for us? It has brought to us not only God's grace and forgiveness for our sins, but the blood of Christ also brings to us the promise and the power of a glorious, redeemed, and regenerated life.

It is a marvelous thing that in the poured out blood of our Lord, we have the poured out blessings of God and of heaven upon us.

The life of our Lord literally was poured out into this world, and that love and grace comes even to us.

When the soldiers smote the Son of God, they struck the rock from which flows the living waters. When they pierced His hands and His feet, they opened the resources of grace, power, and glory from heaven.

When they pierced His side, they opened the fountain of God's love, grace, and mercy. Not only that, but in that gift of God's love in the life of His Son, there came with it that cleansing and regenerating power that makes us new men and women—new creations in God's sight.

THE BLOOD OF CHRIST FOR ME

Have you ever noticed how we categorize sins? Do you see that man over there? He is a violent sinner. Do you see that one over there? He is the dregs of the earth. Do you see that one here? He is as dirt and filth.

We have a tendency to gather our righteous skirts around us and talk about how sinful other people are. Then we remember the Word of the Lord in which God says all have sinned—all. There is not one of us who is righteous by his own means—no, not one. One man may have sinned in one category and another in a different category, but I also have sinned in my categories. My life is full of blemish and wrong, and I need to be saved just as the next person does.

I also need to cast myself upon the mercies of God. I, too, need to say, *"Lord, be merciful to me, a sinner."* Praise God, the same loving grace that was extended to others is extended to me. Under the blood, we all are saved. *"When I see the blood, I will pass over you"* (Ex. 12:13). There is no more condemnation to those who are in Christ Jesus (Rom. 8:1). We are free. We are washed. We are redeemed. We are justified by the blood of the crucified One. I come openly and unashamedly, confessing my faith in the Son of God.

(The writer owes a debt of gratitude to Dr. W. A. Criswell for some of the material regarding the blood of Christ).

WITHOUT SPOT OR BLEMISH

The phrase, *"As of a lamb without blemish and without spot,"* harks back to the lambs which were offered in the old Jewish economy.

At the beginning of the ministry of Christ, John the Baptist used the term, *"Behold the Lamb of God, which takes away the sin of the world"* (Jn. 1:29), when introducing Christ. John, of course, said this at the behest of the Holy Spirit. The meaning is clear.

Of all the untold millions of lambs that had been offered up from the very beginning, starting, it seems, with Abel—at least of which we have an account (Gen., Chpt. 4)—and then increasing greatly with the advent of the sacrificial system in the Levitical law, all, and without exception, typified the coming Son of God. Of course, we are speaking of those offered by God's people. While the blood of bulls and goats could not take away sins, it did serve as a stopgap measure until Christ would come.

As stated, we find the practice beginning with Abel and continued with Noah some 1,600 years later (Gen. 8:20). The practice was taken up by Abraham to such a degree that Abraham was referred to as the altar builder (Gen. 12:8; 13:4; 22:13-14). It was continued by Isaac (Gen. 26:25) and Jacob (Gen. 35:7). Of course, when the Levitical system came into force under Moses, the offering of lambs as sacrifices was constant. Two were offered each day, at 9 A.M. and 3 P.M., with that doubled on the Sabbath.

As well, at the time of the great feasts, especially at Passover, many thousands were offered up. Josephus said that as many as 250,000 were offered during the last Passover week attended by Christ. While not that many, many hundreds, if not thousands, were offered up on the other feast days, as well, during the course of the year. Then again, Israelites were constantly coming and offering up sacrifices. In fact, the altar fires were to never go out on the great brazen altar.

As stated, all of this typified Christ who was to come, and thank God, He has come (Isa., Chpt. 53).

I can see far down the mountain,
Where I have wandered many years,
Often hindered on my journey,
By the ghosts of doubts and fears.

Broken vows and disappointments,
Thickly strewn along the way,
But the Spirit has led unerring,
To the land I hold today.

WHEN I SEE THE BLOOD

CHAPTER 1

THE BEGINNING

CHAPTER ONE

THE BEGINNING

"AND THE LORD SPOKE *unto Moses and Aaron in the land of Egypt saying,*

"This month shall be unto you the beginning of months: it shall be the first month of the year to you" (Ex. 12:1-2).

Chapter 12 of Exodus is a perfect picture of Christ, the true Paschal Lamb.

The Passover was to forever serve as the type of Christ, and it had been kept for nearly 1,600 years when Jesus died on the Cross. Actually, Christ died at 3 P.M., at the exact time the Passover lamb was being offered.

Considering that the blood of bulls and goats could never take away sins, it was not by the sacrifice of these little animals that people were saved, but by having faith in the One whom the sacrifice represented, namely the Lord Jesus Christ. Salvation has always been by faith.

Without a doubt, this makes Chapter 12 of Exodus one of the singular most important chapters in the entirety of the Bible. It ranks with Chapter 4 of Genesis and other similar chapters.

Its vast significance covers much theological area. Not only was the means of deliverance effected for the children of Israel, which extracted them from the clutches of Pharaoh, a type of Satan himself, but, as well, the pattern was drawn as it regarded the coming Redeemer and what he would do as it regarded the salvation of the entirety of mankind. I speak of the Cross and, most of all, the price that Jesus would pay on that wooden gibbet.

DIVINE REVELATION

Another great lesson learned here is the fact that neither Moses nor Aaron introduced any legislation of their own, either at this time or later.

The whole system—spiritual, political, and ecclesiastical—was received by divine revelation, which was commanded by God, and was merely established by the agency of the two brothers. This proclaims the fact that salvation is all of God and none of man. The problem presents itself when man attempts to assert his means and ways into that which God has devised.

Verse 2 proclaims the fact that the month of Abib, which corresponds with our April, became the first month of the year (Abib would later be called "Nisan").

In effect, this tells us that a person doesn't begin to live until he comes to Christ. From that particular time, everything ends, and everything begins. It is actually "the beginning."

I can sense the presence of the Lord even as I dictate these words. How wonderful it is to know the Lord and to have this new life—this eternal life!

I was saved, i.e., born again, at the age of 8. The year was 1943, and I regret very much that I do not remember the month or the day.

SIN

It must, as well, be remembered that the children of Israel were condemned to death just as much as were the Egyptians. The difference was, the children of Israel availed themselves of God's deliverance and redemption plan. When I see the blood ...

Exodus, Chapter 12, records the last of the 10 plagues. This was the death of the firstborn, and inasmuch as death is *"the wages of sin,"* we have no difficulty in perceiving that it is the question of sin that is raised here and with which God deals. This being the case, both the Egyptians and the Israelites alike were obnoxious to God's righteous judgment, for both were sinners before Him. In this respect, the Egyptians and the Israelites were alike: Both in nature and in practice, they were sinners. There is no difference, *"for all have sinned and come short of the glory of God"* (Rom. 3:22-23).

While it is true that God had purposed to redeem Israel out of Egypt, He would do so only on a righteous basis. Holiness can never ignore sin and neither can covenants, no matter where they are found. When the angels sinned,

God spared them not (II Pet. 2:4). The elect are *"children of wrath"* even as others (Eph. 2:3). In fact, God made no exception, even as it regarded His own blessed Son: when He was made *"sin for us"* (II Cor. 5:21), He spared Him not (Rom. 8:32).

A SUBSTITUTE

The further we go into the business of sin, and the more we realize that all fall under its dread yoke, this only seems to make the problem more impossible of solution. The Israelites were sinners; their guilt was irrefutably established. A just God can *"by no means clear the guilty"* (Ex. 34:7). A sentence of death was passed upon them (Ex. 11:5). Nothing remained but the carrying out of the sentence. Why would we go into such detail here as it regards this fact?

A reprieve was out of the question. Justice must be satisfied, and sin must be paid its wages. Human wisdom has no solution, and yet, infinite wisdom says, *"Where sin abounded, grace did much more abound"* (Rom. 5:20). But yet, grace is never extended at the expense of righteousness. We must always remember that. Every demand of justice must be satisfied. Every claim of holiness must be fully met. So, how could it be done?

It can only be done by the means of a substitute. Sentence of death was executed that it fell upon an innocent victim. That which was without blemish died in the stead of those who had no soundness in them (Isa. 1:6).

The difference between the Egyptians and Israel was not a moral difference but was made solely by the blood of the paschal lamb! It was in the blood of the lamb that *mercy and truth met together, and righteousness and peace kissed each other* (Ps. 85:10).

SACRIFICE

Recently, at Family Worship Center, I was actually preaching on the subject of the deliverance of the children of Israel from Egyptian bondage. The Holy Spirit helped me to bring out the point that it was always the sacrifice that was inspected and not the one who brought the sacrifice. It was a foregone conclusion that the offerer of the sacrifice was sinful and wicked. In fact, that was the very purpose and reason for the sacrifice. There was no doubt about that!

Therefore, forgiveness and pardon could never be based upon the righteousness of the sinner, for he had none, so it was the sacrifice that was inspected closely. If it met the criteria and if, in fact, it was accepted, this instantly meant that the offerer of the sacrifice was accepted as well.

When I said those words, the Spirit of God flowed like a river over the congregation as they caught the meaning of what was being said to them.

We are saved and we are kept, not because we are good, but because our faith is in One who was and is good, and I speak of the Lord Jesus Christ. However, it was not His goodness that saved us, not by a long shot, but rather the sacrifice of Himself in the giving and shedding of His own precious blood.

Paul said: *"Who gave Himself for our sins, that He might deliver us from this present evil world, according to the will of God and our Father"* (Gal. 1:4).

THE SACRIFICE OF JESUS CHRIST

Because of its great significance, let me say it again: If the sacrifice is accepted, the sacrificer is accepted as well. If the sacrifice is rejected, the one offering the sacrifice is also rejected.

There is only one sacrifice that's acceptable to God, and that is the sacrifice of His Son and our Saviour, the Lord Jesus Christ. Faith in Him guarantees acceptance by God of our person.

If we reject Him and the price that He paid at Calvary as our substitute, such also guarantees our rejection. That's the reason I preach the Cross so strongly! That's the reason I proclaim the veracity of the shed blood of the Lamb! That's the reason that Paul also said, *"But though we, or an angel from heaven, preach any other gospel unto you than that which we have preached unto you, let him be accursed"* (Gal. 1:8).

A LAMB FOR AN HOUSE

"Speak you unto all the congregation of Israel, saying,

In the tenth day of this month they shall take to them every man a lamb, according to the house of their fathers, a lamb for an house" (Ex. 12:3).

- In Chapter 4 of Genesis, it is a lamb for each person, one might say.
- With Israel being delivered from Egyptian bondage, it was a lamb for each house (Ex. 12:3).
- Upon the giving of the law, it would be a lamb for the entirety of the nation (Lev., Chpt. 16).
- When Jesus came, He would be the Lamb for the entirety of the world.

John said of Him: *"Behold the Lamb of God, which takes away the sin of the world"* (Jn. 1:29).

Why a lamb?

Actually, the Hebrew word used for lamb, *seh*, could be applied equally to sheep or goats.

However, history records that almost without exception, it was lambs that were offered. The Lord is the One who demanded that this type of animal be offered. Under the law, goats, bullocks, heifers, and rams could also be offered, but for the most part, it was lambs.

The lamb represented innocence and gentleness. The prophets represented the tender compassion of God for His people under the figure of the shepherd and the lamb (Isa. 40:11), and, ultimately, the attention of God for His people used the lamb as an important symbol.

THE LAMB

In writing Psalm 23, David carried the imagery of the shepherd and the lamb to its most beautiful expression. Likewise, the lamb was the climax of prophetic symbolism of the suffering of God's people, the servant nation, which the New Testament found to be a prefiguring of Jesus (Isa. 53:7; Acts 8:32). The lamb was a worthy symbol of Jesus who, in innocence, patiently endured suffering as our substitute (I Pet. 1:19). Of special interest is the use of the term *lamb* in the book of Revelation, where it occurs 28 times, all in symbolic reference to Christ.

The introductory reference in Revelation 5:1-14 is to the Lamb triumphant. This description of the Lamb and the works attributed to Him clearly identify Him as the Christ.

The use of the title or the name, Lamb, in the book of Revelation is somewhat different than its use elsewhere in the New Testament. However, it is most likely that it really has the same meaning, a symbolic representation of the redemptive work of Christ, with the added representation of that redemptive work viewed in connection with its triumphant victory over all things.

(The writer is indebted to Drumwright for information respecting the Lamb).

SOULS

"And if the household be too little for the lamb, let him

and his neighbor next unto his house take it according to the number of the souls; every man according to his eating shall make your count for the lamb" (Ex. 12:4).

Several things are said here:

- Every person had to partake. This was mandatory. Because of all the miracles that had been performed, I can hardly think that there would have been even one Israelite who would have been reticent in this.

- As we shall later see, the entirety of the lamb had to be consumed. This has a tremendous spiritual meaning, which we will deal with more fully when we come to Verse 10.

- The whole family was to participate—men, women, and children.

A TYPE OF CHRIST

"Your lamb shall be without blemish, a male of the first year: you shall take it out from the sheep, or from the goats" (Ex. 12:5).

It was fitting that the paschal lamb should be without defect of any kind, especially since it typified the Lamb of God, who is holy, harmless, undefiled—*"a lamb without spot."*

It is said that in later years, after the law was given, each lamb at the morning and evening sacrifices was minutely inspected. In fact, after it was killed, the flesh would be laid open at the backbone and inspected minutely for even a slight discoloration. If so, it would be laid aside and another lamb selected. As stated, this represented Christ and had to be *"without blemish."*

In fact, these particular sacrifices were referred to as *"most holy"* (Lev. 6:17, 25, 29; 7:1, 6; 10:12, 17; 14:13).

THE JESUS DIED SPIRITUALLY DOCTRINE

This debunks the erroneous idea, as proclaimed by some, that Jesus died spiritually on the Cross.

They teach that not only did He die physically, but He died spiritually, as well, which refers to the fact that He, they claim, died as a sinner. They extend His bearing the sin penalty, which He definitely did, to Him actually becoming a sinner, which He did not.

However, several things must be noted: First of all, one cannot be said to be a sinner unless one has sinned, and Jesus Christ never sinned. As stated, by the giving of Himself as a sacrifice on the Cross, He definitely did bear the penalty of sin for the entirety of the world, and for all time.

However, there is a world of difference in bearing the penalty for something and actually being that for which the penalty must be borne.

In fact, had He been a sinner, which means to have sinned even one time, He would have been totally unfit to serve as a sacrifice. He had to be both physically and spiritually *"without blemish,"* which He most definitely was.

They claim that He died as a sinner, went to hell (we speak of the burning side of hell), where he suffered there for three days and three nights, with Satan believing that he had won this conflict. At the end of the three days and three nights, they claim that God said, "It is enough," and Jesus was then "born again," exactly as any sinner is born again.

You will look in vain in the Bible for this foolishness but it simply doesn't exist because it never happened.

THE PENALTY FOR SIN

The death of Christ on the Cross, planned from before the foundation of the world (I Pet. 1:18-20), was meant to pay the penalty of sin, which it did. The shedding of His life's blood (for the life of the flesh is in the blood) guaranteed our salvation, at least for those who will believe (Jn. 3:16). While His death definitely included punishment, it was not punishment that effected our salvation, but rather the paying of the penalty for sin.

"*A male of the first year,*" was meant to portray the virulent manhood of Christ. In other words, He didn't die in the throws of old age, but rather in the prime of manhood.

THE EVENING SACRIFICE

"*And you shall keep it up until the fourteenth day of the same month: and the whole assembly of the congregation of Israel shall kill it in the evening*" (Ex. 12:6).

On the tenth day, they were to select the lamb, and then on the 14TH day, it was to be killed.

During the intervening four days, they were to inspect the animal minutely and make certain that it was without blemish.

Each house was to kill the little animal in the evening. This corresponded with the time of the evening sacrifice, which was at 3 P.M., which would later be enacted.

This was the time that Jesus died on the Cross—3 P.M.

THE BLOOD

"And they shall take of the blood, and strike it on the two side posts and on the upper door post of the houses, wherein they shall eat it" (Ex. 12:7).

The whole value of the blood of the paschal lamb lay in its being a type of the Lord Jesus—*"Christ our Passover is sacrificed for us: therefore let us keep the feast"* (I Cor. 5:7-8).

Here is divine authority for our regarding the contents of Exodus, Chapter 12, as typical of the Cross-work of our blessed Saviour. It is this that invests every detail of our chapter with such deep interest.

Pink said, "May our eyes be anointed so that we shall be able to perceive some, at least, of the precious unfolding of the truths which are typically set forth in this great chapter."

At this time, the blood, which represented the shed blood of Christ, was to be put on the side posts and the upper posts of the house. Later, it would be applied to the mercy seat on the Great Day of Atonement. Now, by faith, it is applied to our hearts (Jn. 3:16).

The blood applied to the doorways is probably to be connected to the idea that the secondary agency producing death, whatever it was, would enter by the door. If the door showed atonement for the house, it would not enter.

GOD'S ETERNAL PURPOSE IN CHRIST

Concerning all of this, Mackintosh said:

> Now, the lamb taken on the tenth day, and kept up until the fourteenth day, shows us Christ foreordained of God from eternity, but manifest for us in time. God's eternal purpose in Christ becomes the foundation of the believer's peace. Nothing short of this would do.
>
> We are carried back far beyond creation, beyond the bounds of time, beyond the entrance in of sin and everything that could possibly affect the groundwork of our peace. The expression, 'foreordained before the foundation of the world,' as Peter used the term, conducts us back into the unfathomed depths of eternity, and shows us God forming His own counsels of redeeming love, and basing them all upon the atoning blood of His own precious, spotless Lamb. Christ was ever the primary thought in the divine mind; and hence, the moment He began to speak or act, He took occasion to shadow forth that One who occupied the highest place in His

counsels and affections; and, as we pass along the current inspiration, we find that every ceremony, every rite, every ordinance, and every sacrifice pointed forward to 'the Lamb of God that takes away the sin of the world,' and not one more strikingly than the Passover. The paschal lamb, with all the attendant circumstances, forms one of the most profoundly interesting and deeply instructive types of Scripture.

THE FAMILY

The family gathered around the lamb, even as we will see in the following verses, and partook of this particular Feast, i.e., "the Passover." This presents a picture of the church, gathered by the Holy Spirit, all in the name of Jesus. The entirety of the Bible is about Christ, and more particularly, what Christ did in order to redeem lost humanity and, as well, to satisfy the righteousness and justice of a thrice-holy God. The Cross, as we will later see, had a twofold effect. It was both man-ward and God-ward.

BITTER HERBS

"And they shall eat the flesh in that night, roast with fire, and unleavened bread; and with bitter herbs they shall eat it" (Ex. 12:8).

The eating the flesh pertains to the words of Christ when He said: *"I am the living bread which came down from heaven: if any man eat of this bread, he shall live forever: and the bread that I will give is My flesh, which I will give for the life of the world."*

He then said: *"Except you eat the flesh of the Son of Man, and drink His blood, you have no life in you.*

"Whoso eats My flesh, and drinks My blood, has eternal life" (Jn. 6:51, 53-54).

What did Jesus mean by all of this?

He would momentarily ask the question, *"Does this offend you?"*

He then said: *"It is the Spirit who quickens* (makes alive); *the flesh profits nothing: the words that I speak unto you, they are spirit, and they are life"* (Jn. 6:61, 63).

By using this terminology, Jesus was speaking of the death He would die on the Cross by the giving of Himself, i.e., *the flesh,* and the blood that He would shed.

THE CROSS

In essence, we eat His flesh and drink His blood when we evidence faith in what He did at the Cross. When such faith is evidenced, in the mind of God, the believer is literally baptized into the death of Christ, buried with Him, and raised with Him in newness of life (Rom. 6:3-5).

It is far more than a mere mental acceptance or even a philosophical acceptance of something. Faith puts us into Christ and what He did for us, which the eating of the lamb of the Passover represented.

The Passover represented salvation in that we were delivered from the powers of darkness to the Lord of Glory. However, if it is to be noticed, the sacrificial system did not begin and end with the Passover.

In fact, there were five different sacrificial offerings instituted in the law of Moses. All of them, with the exception of one (the meat, food, or thank offering), pertained to the shedding of blood.

So, what are we saying?

We are saying that exactly as the sinner is to look to Christ and the Cross for salvation, likewise, the believer is to continue to look to Christ and the Cross as it regards our sanctification.

HOW TO LIVE FOR GOD

A short time ago, I made the statement over our daily telecast, *The Message Of The Cross*, that most believers simply do not know how to live for God. I realize the statement is controversial, but still, it happens to be true.

The way to properly live for God according to the Word of God can perhaps be described in the following brief (very brief) formula:

- Focus: Christ and Him crucified (Rom. 6:1-14).
- Object of faith: the finished work of Christ (Col. 2:10-15).
- Power source: the Holy Spirit (Rom. 8:1-11).
- Results: perpetual victory (I Cor. 1:17, 18, 23; 2:2).

Regrettably, that which we have given is little taught and understood in most churches, with the following rather being the manner in which most believers are trying to live for God:

- Focus: Works.
- Object of faith: Performance.
- Power source: Self.
- Results: Perpetual defeat.

Paul addressed this by saying, *"But now we are delivered from the law* (from its penalty by and through the death of Christ), *that being dead wherein we were held; that we should serve in newness of Spirit, and not in the oldness of the letter* (the law)" (Rom. 7:6).

The first diagram I gave pertains to the *"newness of spirit."* The second pertains to the *"oldness of the letter."*

God has one way of salvation, which is Jesus Christ and Him crucified (I Cor. 1:23). He also has one way of victory for the saint, and that is *"Jesus Christ, and Him crucified"* (I Cor. 2:2).

As is obvious, it is the same for both salvation and sanctification.

DO YOU UNDERSTAND THE CROSS OF CHRIST?

In fact, the Cross of Christ is the simplest system in the world. Concerning this, Paul said, *"But I fear, lest by any means, as the serpent beguiled Eve through his subtilty, so your minds should be corrupted from the simplicity that is in Christ"* (II Cor. 11:3).

The Cross is not simple to some simply because their minds are cluttered with all types of false doctrine. Please understand, all false ways are connected with unbelief.

The truth is, most Christians are functioning in law even though they do not really understand that to be the case. In fact, there are only two places that a believer can position himself spiritually. It is either grace or law.

If our faith is in anything except Jesus Christ and Him crucified, then whether we realize it or not, we are functioning in law. The way that we function in grace is that our faith is placed exclusively in Christ and the Cross, and maintained exclusively in Christ and the Cross.

As it regards grace, regrettably, many Christians have the idea that because this is the dispensation of grace, and it definitely is, this means that we are automatically under grace. It doesn't!

Paul also said, *"I do not frustrate the grace of God: for if righteousness come by the law, then Christ is dead in vain"* (Gal. 2:21).

The apostle said several things in this one passage.

First of all, he informed us that it is definitely possible to *"frustrate the grace of God,"* which means to hinder its flow or to stop it altogether.

So, if it is possible to frustrate the grace of God, and it definitely is, how is such done?

Whenever we seek to bring about righteousness by law of any nature, we frustrate the grace of God. Let us say it another way: As we have stated, if your faith is not exclusively in Christ and the Cross, this means that your faith is in law, whether you understand such or not. This frustrates the grace of God because it is the Cross of Christ that makes all grace possible (Rom. 6:14).

THEN CHRIST IS DEAD IN VAIN

To make it simpler, this refers to Christians doing certain good things or not doing certain bad things, which they think make them righteous. Paul here bluntly tells us that such activity can never bring about righteousness. In fact, all the good things in the world, whatever they might be, cannot fall out to righteousness. As Paul goes on to say, if it could bring about righteousness, *"then Christ is dead in vain,"* meaning that Jesus died needlessly on the Cross.

However, the truth is, He did not needlessly die on a Cross. He did so simply because there was no way that man could make himself righteous. In fact, righteousness can only come in one manner and one way. That is by the believer, as stated, evidencing faith totally and completely in Christ and what Christ has done for us at the Cross. When this is done, righteousness is automatically imputed to the individual.

Paul said, *"For by grace are you saved through faith; and that not of yourselves* (not by keeping laws, etc.): *it is the gift of God: Not of works, lest any man should boast"* (Eph. 2:8-9).

To know how to be saved is one thing, but to know how to live for God after one is saved is something else altogether.

As someone has well said, "The glad tidings of salvation is one thing; the struggle against the power that tries to keep the soul in bondage is quite another."

If it is to be noticed, there is very little information given in the Word of God as it regards the sinner being saved. To be sure, there are plenty of passages that inform us of this great truth (Rom. 10:9-10, 13; Rev. 22:17; Jn. 3:16). However, the greater bulk of the Word of God (over 99 percent) is given over to telling the believer how to live for God. This culminates with that which was given to the Apostle Paul, which he gave to us in his 14 epistles.

JUDGMENT

The lamb was to be roasted with fire, which typified the judgment of God that would come upon Christ instead of coming upon us. That is the God-ward part that Calvary produced. The man-ward part pertains to what the Cross made possible, and I speak of the advent of the Holy Spirit. In other words, due to Christ atoning for all sin, which means the sin debt in its totality is paid, the Holy Spirit can now take up permanent residence within the heart and life of any believer (Jn. 14:16-17).

The Holy Spirit is also represented by fire, which symbolizes that which Calvary effects—the cleansing and purification of the saint. The Cross satisfied the righteousness and justice of God and, at the same time, makes the believer a fit subject for the kingdom of God.

UNLEAVENED BREAD

This made typical the fact that Christ was and is perfect. He was perfect in His humanity in every respect, hence, being worthy as a perfect sacrifice. Leaven is used in the Bible as representing sin and imperfection. The bread that was to be used in the Passover contained no leaven, proclaiming the fact that Jesus would have no sin. As we've already stated, had there been sin in Him in any capacity, He would not have been an acceptable sacrifice. Only a perfect sacrifice could satisfy the righteousness of God.

To the man-ward side, this portrays the fact that the believer can, as well, live such a life that sin will not have dominion over him (Rom. 6:14).

BITTER HERBS

The bitter herbs were to remind the children of Israel of the slavery that they experienced in Egypt (Ex. 1:14).

Bringing it up to these times in which we now live, the believer must understand that we have been saved out of a life of spiritual bondage, which makes life a little bit of hell on earth.

There is a certain young Hollywood singer and actress who is well known all over the world and is making millions of dollars each year. I heard a reporter ask her why she did some of the things that she did that put her in hot water with the law, etc. Among other things, her children had been taken from her several times. Her reply was most interesting. She said, "You ask me why I do these things, and I will tell you: Life is so boring."

Now, think about that for a moment. She had everything that money could buy, plus fame and popularity, but still, she said that life was so boring. She was right! It was and is, at least whenever we try to live it without God.

There is an emptiness in man who doesn't know the Lord. That emptiness cannot be satisfied with anything but God. Money cannot satisfy the situation, and neither can power or prestige satisfy the situation. In fact, nothing can satisfy except Jesus Christ.

As someone has well said, "The soul of man is so big that only God can fill it up."

THE PURTENANCE

"Eat not of it raw, nor sodden at all with water, but roast with fire; his head with his legs, and with the purtenance thereof" (Ex. 12:9).

The purtenance pertained to the intestines, which were removed and washed and then placed back in the animal. As is obvious here, they were to be eaten when the lamb was consumed.

(Some claim that the intestines were not included here, but rather the heart, liver, and kidneys; however, it probably did include the intestines as well.)

"Eat not of it raw" has two meanings:

1. The Egyptians ate raw flesh in honor of one of their gods, Osiris. Thus, God was seeking to impress upon Israel that Egyptian practices must not be included in the instructions given concerning this all-important feast.

2. The *"roast with fire,"* as we've already stated, spoke of the finished work of Christ in taking upon Himself the judgment intended for us.

CHRIST WITHOUT THE CROSS
AFFORDS NO SALVATION

Let's say it another way: It speaks of the fact that when Christ is accepted minus the Cross, it affords no salvation. Regrettably, this is the condition in which much of the modern church world now finds itself. Calvary has been placed in a subservient position, if any position at all.

In fact, the Word of Faith doctrine, in reality, is no faith at all, at least that God will accept, yet, it has made great inroads into Pentecostal, Charismatic, and some Baptist churches. However, it openly repudiates the Cross, referring to it as "the greatest defeat in human history."

Consequently, in many of their churches, songs about the blood, the Cross, the sacrifice, and the price that Jesus paid are not allowed to be sung. So, the error of these churches and these preachers is the worst error of all. To misunderstand anything as it regards the Word of God always has a negative effect; however, to misunderstand the atonement is to misunderstand the very heart of the gospel. One can be saved and still, at the same time, believe many erroneous things; however, one cannot be saved and have a misunderstanding of the atonement, and we speak of disavowing the Cross.

So, the lamb had to be *"roasted with fire,"* typifying the death that Christ would die on the Cross, of which the altar was ever a type.

ALL OF CHRIST IS TO BE ACCEPTED

"And you shall let nothing of it remain until the morning; and that which remains of it until the morning you shall burn with fire" (Ex. 12:10).

Let's look at what is being said:

- All of the lamb must be eaten.
- Whatever was left concerning bones and fragments was to be burned with fire.

All of this tells us the following:

- Christ would give His all for us, and we are to give our all for Him.
- One must accept all of Christ, or one cannot have any of Christ.

There are millions of Christians who want the prosperity Christ, but they don't want the Christ of the Cross. There are others who want the salvation Christ, but not Christ the baptizer with the Holy Spirit.

However, the Scripture is emphatic. Christ is to be accepted in totality, and above all, *"Jesus Christ and Him crucified"* is to be accepted. To accept Christ as merely a great teacher, a great miracle worker, a great provider regarding material things, or even a great healer, and yet, refuse to accept Christ and the Cross is plainly forbidden here. It's all or nothing!

THE CROSS

In fact, the only way that one can have Christ the healer, Christ the provider, Christ the miracle worker, etc., is to have Christ the Saviour, which speaks of the Cross.

To vividly portray Calvary, not only must the animal be roasted with fire, but, as well, as stated, even the scraps were to be burned and consumed with fire.

Last of all, it had to be eaten at one sitting. Nothing was to be allowed to "remain until the morning," meaning that a second meal would not be prepared, etc.

This tells us that Christ cannot be received in stages. He can only be received in totality.

To use a crude example, it's not possible for a woman to be partially pregnant, and neither can one partially accept Christ. Once again, it's all or nothing.

THE LORD'S PASSOVER

"And thus shall you eat it; with your loins girded, your shoes on your feet, and your staff in your hand; and you shall eat it in haste: it is the LORD's Passover" (Ex. 12:11).

The loins girded, the shoes on the feet, and the staff in the hand proclaim the fact that they were leaving. Egypt was to be put behind them, and Canaanland was to beckon.

The same admonition holds true for the modern believer and, in fact, all believers who have ever lived. Even though we have been saved out of this world, we are still in the world. We eagerly await the moment when the trump of God shall sound and, thereby, rapture us away (I Thess. 4:13-18).

After the law was given, and Israel was safely ensconced in the Promised Land, they were to eat the Passover resting— for all the obvious reasons. However, the type still holds as it regards modern believers and our awaiting the rapture of the church.

Jesus said, *"Watch therefore, for you know neither the day nor the hour wherein the Son of Man comes"* (Mat. 25:13).

If it is to be noticed, it is referred to as *"the Lord's Passover."*

This emphasizes a side of the truth that is much neglected today in evangelical preaching.

TO GLORIFY GOD

What little is presently preached about the Cross is, for the most part, one-sided. It has much to say about what Christ's death accomplished for those who believe in Him, and rightly so; however, very little is said about what that death accomplished God-ward.

Concerning this, Pink said, "The death of Christ glorified God if never a single sinner had been saved by the virtue of it."

He then went on to say, "The more we study the teaching of Scripture on this subject, and the more we lay hold by simple faith of what the Cross meant to God, the more stable will be our peace, and the deeper our joy and praise."

As we survey the first time in Scripture that there is a direct reference to the word *lamb*, we read that Abraham said to Isaac, *"God will provide Himself a lamb for a burnt offering"* (Gen. 22:8). It was not simply that God would provide a lamb, but that He would provide Himself a lamb. The lamb was provided to glorify God's character—to vindicate His throne, to satisfy His justice, and to magnify His holiness.

Then, on the Great Day of Atonement, which came about once a year, we read of two goats. Why two?

One was to portray justice satisfied, with the other goat portraying redemption completed. The latter was the "scapegoat."

JUSTIFICATION

It is this aspect of truth that is before us in Romans 3:24-26, *"Being justified freely by His grace through the redemption that is in Christ Jesus. Whom God has set forth to be a 'propitiation' through faith in His blood, to declare His 'righteousness' ... that He might be 'just,' and* the 'Justifier' of him who believes in Jesus."

In I Corinthians 5:7, we read, "*Christ our Passover.*" He is now our Passover because He was first *"the LORD's Passover"* (Ex. 12:11).

THE CROSS AND SATAN

As we have stated, the Cross was meant to address itself to both man and God. It would satisfy the justice of God, and it would redeem man.

The Cross had absolutely nothing to do with Satan, even though the Cross, or at least what was accomplished there, totally and completely defeated him, as well as all of his minions of darkness.

Paul said:

"*Blotting out the handwriting of ordinances that was against us* (satisfied the demands of the broken law), *which was contrary to us* (man could not keep the law), *and took it out of the way* (satisfied its demands by paying its debt), *nailing it to His Cross* (atonement was totally and completely effected at the Cross);

"*And having spoiled principalities and powers* (by Jesus atoning for all sin, and with sin being the legal claim that Satan had over humanity, with that removed, he has no more claim, at least for all who will believe) *He made a show of them openly* (all of the spirit world knows that

Christ is victor), *triumphing over them in it* (by what Christ did at the Cross, Satan and his demons were totally defeated)" (Col. 2:14-15).

ALL WAS ACCOMPLISHED AT THE CROSS

This is the reason that Satan hates the Cross. It spelled his doom, wrote "finished" over his efforts, took away his claims, and left him nothing. Let me say it again: All was accomplished at the Cross. That's the reason that Paul said: *"For Christ sent me not to baptize, but to preach the gospel: not with wisdom of words, lest the Cross of Christ should be made of none effect"* (I Cor. 1:17).

This tells us here several things:

- The emphasis must always be on the Cross. If it's on anything else, as important as those other things might be, then it becomes unscriptural.
- We are told in this one verse that the gospel is *"Jesus Christ and Him crucified."*

We are also told that men are not saved by appealing to the intellect, i.e., *"wisdom of words,"* but rather by God dealing with their hearts as the Cross of Christ is preached.

- Last of all, the Cross can be *"made of none effect"* simply because emphasis is placed elsewhere, which then destroys the effectiveness of the gospel.

As well, the Jew from Tarsus said, *"But we preach Christ crucified,"* meaning that we must not just preach Christ, but we must preach Christ crucified (I Cor. 1:23).

We are to preach the Cross despite the fact that it is *"unto the Jews a stumblingblock, and unto the Greeks foolishness"* (I Cor. 1:23). None of this must deter us!

The reason?

The Cross of Christ makes possible the *"power of God, and the wisdom of God"* (I Cor. 1:24).

I AM THE LORD

"For I will pass through the land of Egypt this night, and will smite all the firstborn in the land of Egypt, both man and beast; and against all the gods of Egypt I will execute judgment: I am the LORD" (Ex. 12:12).

It must be understood that in respect to personal holiness, the children of Israel were no different than the Egyptians. The difference would be the applied blood.

"When I see the blood, I will pass over you" are, no doubt, the greatest words that were ever uttered.

The shed blood of Jesus Christ is the only panacea for the plague of sin that destroys the human race.

Blood applied gave security to the home. Doubt by the occupants might have destroyed the peace but not the security because the security was founded on God's Word.

The Passover was to be *"for a memorial"* and was to be kept forever. The Lord's Supper of Christianity is an outgrowth of the Passover and, thereby, fulfills the command. There is some indication that the Passover and other memorials will be kept forever, or at least through the kingdom age

(Ezek. 45:17; 46:14).

The words *passed through* could be translated "go through" since the word used is entirely unconnected with the Passover. By now, Egypt had come to recognize Jehovah and to recognize fully that His power was and is almighty.

Actually, Jehovah did not personally go through the land of Egypt that particular night, but rather sent the death angel, which is referred to as *"the destroyer"* (Ex. 12:23).

ANIMAL WORSHIP

We may wonder why the beasts would be included.

Animal worship was an important part of the religion of the Egyptians. At four great cities—Memphis, Heliopolis, Hermonthis, a sort of suburb of Thebes; and Momemphis in the western delta—animals were maintained, which were viewed as actual incarnations of deity: the Apis bull at Memphis, a bull called Mnevis at Heliopolis, one termed Bacis or Pacis at Hermonthis, and a white cow at Momemphis.

In other parts of Egypt, sheep were worshipped as well as goats, and even dogs and cats. Crocodiles and hippopotami were included, as well, along with frogs.

A sudden mortality among the sacred animals would be felt by the Egyptians as a blow struck against the gods to whom they belonged and as a judgment upon them. In fact, many of the gods of Egypt were represented by some beast.

Even above all of that, with the firstborn of each family in Egypt being smitten, including the family of Pharaoh, it struck a blow at Egypt of unprecedented proportions.

As previously stated, the religion of Egypt included the firstborn taking on the name and the ability, even into eternity, or the "afterlife," as it was called. So, when the firstborn prematurely died, this affected the eternal consequences of that particular family.

So, the Lord would execute judgment against all the gods of Egypt simply because He alone was "the LORD," and not these supposed deities.

THE BLOOD

"And the blood shall be to you for a token upon the houses where you are: and when I see the blood, I will pass over you, and the plague shall not be upon you to destroy you, when I smite the land of Egypt" (Ex. 12:13).

In this chapter, which is one of the greatest in the Bible, we now come to the particular verse that is the most important in this chapter. In this verse, the one phrase, *"When I see the blood, I will pass over you,"* in effect, constitutes one of the most important statements in the entirety of the Bible. In fact, it sums up the entirety of the Word of God.

THE ONLY THING THAT COUNTED
WAS THE BLOOD

It didn't matter if the house was beautiful, expensive, ornate, or the poorest of poor structures. None of that counted. The only thing that counted was the blood that was applied to the doorposts. That's what the Lord saw, and that only.

Again, as it regarded the individuals in these respective houses, it didn't matter that they could trace their lineage back to Abraham, that their genealogy was perfect, or that they observed all the ceremonies. That which secured their deliverance was not these things, but rather their personal application of the shed blood, and that alone.

The blood applied to the doorposts meant that their faith and trust were in the paschal lamb. They may not have understood very much about what was taking place, but this one thing they did know: if they were to be safe on this memorable night, the blood had to be applied to the doorposts, and that was all that mattered.

PERSONAL APPLICATION

No doubt, there were some in these houses who had not lived as properly as they should have lived. Perhaps fear filled their hearts because they knew that they deserved the death penalty.

However, they had heard the Word of the Lord from Moses, and that Word had been, *"When I see the blood, I will pass over you."* The lamb had taken the fatal blow, and because it had taken the blow, the one in the house would be spared. It was not a question of personal worthiness. Self had nothing whatever to do in the matter. It was a matter of faith, and all under the cover of the blood were safe, just as all presently under the cover of the blood are safe.

This means that they were not merely in a savable state, but rather that they were "saved." They were not hoping or praying to be saved; they knew it as an assured fact on the authority of that Word which shall endure throughout all generations.

As well, they were not partly saved and partly exposed to judgment; they were wholly saved because there is no such thing as a partial justification. The blood of the lamb and the Word of the Lord formed the foundation of Israel's peace on that terrible night in which Egypt's firstborns were laid low.

THE VERY HEART OF CHRISTIANITY

Even though the words *Christians* and *Christianity* were at that time unknown, still, what we are studying here is the very heart of Christianity. It's what true Christianity is all about. It's the story of the Bible because, in effect, it's the story of the Cross.

Satan does everything within his power to obscure this foundational truth from humanity and even the church. Religious men are so very bad—awful, in fact—about adding things to the finished work of Christ.

They seem to not realize that when this is done, they are insulting Christ with the most awful of insults.

They are, in effect, saying that what He did at the Cross is insufficient, and to be sure, such thinking borders very close to blasphemy, if not outright blasphemy.

If we do not see the absolutely settled character of redemption through the blood of Christ in its application to ourselves, then we are not aware of full forgiveness, grace, and mercy simply because full forgiveness rests upon the simple fact that a full and complete atonement has been offered.

We either trust it, or we don't trust it!

FAITH IN THE SHED BLOOD OF THE LORD JESUS CHRIST

When we claim to trust Christ but, at the same time, add our particular church, doctrine, or good works to that finished work, we have only succeeded in abrogating the great plan of God in our lives. Nothing could be more serious than that. However, I'm afraid that this is the state of the majority of the modern church.

How do I know that?

I know that because of the attitude and position taken by many, if not most, church leaders, which are followed by most of the laity. What attitude is that?

Simple repentance for sin is not enough for most church leaders—so-called leaders! In fact, most of the modern church believes in and practices penance, although most would probably deny such a position.

Of course, penance loudly says that what Christ did at the Cross is not enough, and we have to add our effort to the Cross. As stated, this is blasphemy!

A PERSONAL EXPERIENCE

A friend of mine, who is an attorney, was discussing these things with the leader of one of the largest Pentecostal denominations in the world.

He told me that after he left and was thinking about their conversation, he realized that what this man was advocating was penance.

The Catholic Church openly advocates penance, and even though the Protestant world would blanch at the word, still, for the most part, it practices the same thing. Let the reader understand that penance, which, in effect, is punishment, is an insult to Christ of unprecedented proportions. In effect, it states that the terrible price that He paid at the Cross was not enough and needs more punishment added.

WHEN I SEE THE BLOOD, I WILL PASS OVER YOU

Let me ask this question: What if it had been prescribed by some that Israelites also stand on their heads in their homes, and I speak of the night that the death angel passed through? Would their performing this particular acrobatic feat have made them any safer? Let's also say that it was recommended that they stay on their knees all night long. Would this have made them safer?

I think we all know the answer to that. None of that, irrespective of what it might have been, would have been looked at by the Lord. He was looking for one thing, and that was the blood applied to the doorposts. Anything else that was proposed would have been ignored.

It is the same presently. The word that He gave some 3,500 years ago, *"When I see the blood, I will pass over you,"* holds true at this present hour as much as it did then and more. Why can't we see that? Why don't we believe that? Why don't we preach that? Why would we try to add other things to that great promise?

If your faith and trust is in Christ and Him crucified then you are saved, and there is nothing you can do to make yourself more saved.

SELF

There are millions of Christians, and I think I exaggerate not, who claim to believe totally in the shed blood of Christ, but yet, they have no peace. In fact, the great blessing of faith in the shed blood of Christ is the peace of God that floods one's soul. So, what's wrong?

While these individuals claim to be looking to the blood, the truth is, they are looking to themselves. They are occupied with their interests and their faith instead of Christ's blood and God's Word. In other words, they are looking in at self instead of out at Christ. This is not faith, and as a consequence, they have no peace.

For the most part, the ways of God are totally opposite to the ways of this world. With God, the way up is down. With God, we keep what we give. With God, if we save our lives, we will lose them, etc. I think you get the point.

ONE OF THE GREAT KEYS TO VICTORY

What I'm about to say to you, that is, if the Lord will help me to say it properly, is, in fact, a great truth that can bring you victory. It is the key to victory.

We have a tendency to measure our victory by looking at ourselves. When we do this, it's going to cause us problems. We are to always look to Christ and what Christ has done for us at the Cross. I am saved and my name is written in the Lamb's Book of Life, not because of my excellent performance, but because of Christ and what He has done for me at the Cross and my faith in that finished work.

However, after we are saved, we realize that our performance should shape up, and that is correct, but the way to worsen the condition is to keep looking at yourself and, thereby, devising means and ways to be an overcomer, etc. That is the sure road to disaster simply because it's not faith.

Please note the following very carefully: If you will forget about yourself, look exclusively to Christ, and measure your victory according to what Christ has done for you, you will find something beginning to take place in your life.

THE OBJECT OF ONE'S FAITH

As you begin this great quest, with your faith being imperfect, you will probably fail in some way. If that happens, as despicable as it is, ask the Lord to forgive you and then get your faith anchored once again in Christ and the Cross. It's just a matter of believing, but believing the right thing. In fact, this might happen several times, even many times. Irrespective of that, don't look at yourself, and above all, don't look at your poor performance; rather look to Christ and His Cross. Why do you think that Paul said, *"God forbid that I should glory* (boast), *save in the Cross of our Lord Jesus Christ, by whom the world is crucified unto me, and I unto the world"* (Gal. 6:14)?

Instead of boasting in yourself or doing the very opposite, which means to chastise yourself because of your failures, rather look to the Cross and understand that Jesus was punished for us. Your punishing yourself over and over again, or anytime at all, is not going to be of any help, but rather harm. You should rather look to the Cross and boast about that great finished work performed there by Christ. You will find yourself little by little getting stronger and stronger, and the time will definitely come that the problems causing you great difficulty will no longer be there.

RULES WHICH WE DEVISE

To fail the Lord in any capacity is a hurtful thing. In fact, every true Christian hates sin with a passion. However, we sin because we do not realize God's way, which is the Cross, or else, we take our eyes off that great sacrifice for a period of time. With that being done, failure will always be the result.

The way to overcome what is causing failure is not through self but exclusively through Christ. Unfortunately, most Christians do not understand the Cross, which means they do not properly understand justification. Therefore, if they fail, they automatically concoct particular laws or rules of their own making, or the making of someone else, which they think will bring them victory.

To be sure, religious man loves to make up rules, and he loves to try to force other people to obey them. Please understand, it is possible to make a law out of almost anything, but then we find to our chagrin that these things do not bring victory. In fact, if the truth be known, the situation rather gets worse, and that's the way it always is. If we are trying to live under the government of law, whether we realize it's the government of law or not, failure, and continued failure, is going to be our lot. It is because the Holy Spirit will not help us in such capacities simply because, as previously stated, we are actually committing spiritual adultery whether we realize it or not. We are married to Christ, but at the same time, we are flirting with the law, or else, have embraced the law. So, in effect, to use strictly street terminology, we have two husbands, Christ and the law. This makes us a spiritual adulterer, which the Holy Spirit cannot tolerate (Rom. 7:1-4).

AN OVERCOMER

To the seven churches of Asia, Jesus addressed seven messages (Rev., Chpts. 2-3). In each of these seven messages,

He made a statement concerning believers being overcomers. While each statement is different, He strongly implies that we must be overcomers.

When reading these statements, what do you think as it regards yourself and your position as an overcomer? Do you think of yourself as an overcomer, or do you think in your mind that this is something on which you are working?

Better yet, were I to ask how the believer could be an overcomer, what would your answer be?

The Scripture says: *"And they overcame him* (Satan) *by the blood of the Lamb, and by the word of their testimony; and they loved not their lives unto the death"* (Rev. 12:11).

When most believers think of overcoming, they think of themselves as doing something, ceasing to do something, etc. No! The Scripture plainly says that we overcome by the *"blood of the Lamb."* What does that mean?

It refers to faith. Paul said, *"For in Jesus Christ neither circumcision avails anything, nor uncircumcision; but faith which works by love"* (Gal. 5:6).

We overcome simply by placing our faith and trust in Christ and what Christ has done for us at the Cross, knowing that He shed His life's blood there, which atoned for all sin and, as well, defeated Satan and all his cohorts. When faith is properly registered in Christ, and it can't be properly registered in Him unless it is also registered in what He did for us at the Cross, we will then have the help of the Holy Spirit, and victory will be ours (Rom. 8:1-11).

Our being an overcomer is not in what we do, but rather

what He has done and our faith in Him. Of course, I speak of Christ. That's the reason the loud voice from heaven cried that we overcome Satan by the *"blood of the Lamb."* Get your eyes off your failures and get them onto His perfection.

THE WORD OF OUR TESTIMONY

The loud voice from heaven also stated that we overcome not only by the *"blood of the Lamb"* but also *"by the word of our testimony."* What is meant by that?

It simply means that our testimony is to the effect of the very things I've been saying here. We are to testify that our faith is exclusively in Christ and what He has done for us in His great sacrifice. That is our testimony and must ever be our testimony. If it changes, and I speak of it changing from the blood of Christ to other things, then it's a testimony that God will not honor or recognize.

Our testimony is tied to the blood of the Lamb. That's where our faith is registered, and whenever we speak of victory, without exception, we must speak of Christ and Him crucified. That is the word of our testimony.

TOKEN

"And the blood shall be to you for a token upon the houses where you are ..." (Ex. 12:13).

Token in the Hebrew is *owth* and means "a flag, beacon, monument, evidence." Probably the word *evidence* would explain this more than anything else.

The blood on the doorposts was evidence of their faith in that which was commanded of them.

To the mind of the natural man, this was consummate folly. "What difference will it make," proud reason might ask, "if 'blood' be smeared upon the door?"

That's the reason that Paul said: *"For the preaching (message) of the Cross is to them who perish foolishness; but unto us who are saved it is the power of God."*

He also stated, *"But we preach Christ crucified, unto the Jews a stumblingblock, and unto the Greeks foolishness"* (I Cor. 1:18, 23).

It is faith, not reasoning, that God requires; and it was faith that rendered the Passover sacrifice effective: *"Through faith he kept the Passover, and the sprinkling of blood, lest He who destroyed the firstborn should touch them"* (Heb. 11:28).

Some nine miracles or plagues had come and gone, and the children of Israel were still held captive by Pharaoh. So, how could this last plague make any difference?

THE DIFFERENCE

It was different because the power of God struck at the very heart of the Egyptian Empire by bringing about the deaths of all the firstborn, both man and beasts. When this took place—and take place it did—Pharaoh relented, but it was just long enough for the children of Israel to leave. He would come after them, which would prove to be his undoing.

How does all of this tie in with our present salvation?

Presently, as then, our salvation is centered up in the blood of the Lamb. When Jesus died on the Cross, thereby, shedding His life's blood, which atoned for all sin, this took away Satan's legal right to hold man in bondage. Sin is what gave him that legal right, but with all sin now atoned, it left him with nothing.

That's why Paul said: *"Blotting out the handwriting of ordinances that was against us, which was contrary to us, and took it out of the way, nailing it to His Cross; and having spoiled principalities and powers, He made a show of them openly, triumphing over them in it"* (Col. 2:14-15).

So, the question might be asked, "If Satan has lost his legal right to keep mankind in bondage, at least regarding those who believe, how is it that he's still causing so much trouble for many Christians?"

SATAN'S PSEUDO-AUTHORITY

Satan exercises control over Christians through a pseudo-authority. What do we mean by that?

It means that he really doesn't have any authority except that which we give him.

Now, that may come as a shock, and I speak of our giving him authority, which he then turns and uses against us.

Again I state, he has no authority of his own, that having been addressed at Calvary. So, if he exercises authority now, it has to be a pseudo-authority.

When it comes to the unsaved, of course, he exercises authority over them constantly, but once again, that is a pseudo-authority as well. They don't trust Christ, so that gives Satan an opening in their lives, which he uses to the full extent.

When it comes to Christians, it is by and large the same thing. If the Christian doesn't understand what Christ has done at the Cross and how His great finished work brings about our sanctification, this falls right into Satan's hands. We are speaking of Christians not understanding how we live for God and, thereby, are trying to bring victory in some other way. In other words, we have left the gate open.

Satan then takes the authority we aren't using, whether through ignorance or otherwise, and uses it against us to cause us all kinds of problems. However, if the believer will exercise his authority, then Satan has no authority whatsoever and is a defeated foe. When we speak of exercising authority, we are speaking in the sense of evidencing faith in Christ and what Christ has done for us in the great sacrifice of Himself. We must realize that this alone brings about total and complete victory. Never forget that the triumph of Jesus over Satan and all his cohorts was final, total, and complete.

A COMPLETE VICTORY

The Scripture plainly says that Jesus *"made a show of them openly, triumphing over them in it"* (Col. 2:15), which

He did by His accomplishment at the Cross. Satan knows he's defeated, but the sadness is, most Christians don't!

Oh, yes! Almost every Christian will talk about how Satan is defeated, but most of the time, their thinking is in themselves and not in the Cross.

In other words, they're boasting of themselves and not boasting of Christ (Gal. 6:14).

Exactly as the children of Israel of old, the blood is a token where we are, referring to the fact of the Cross and what Jesus accomplished there.

That's why Paul also said, *"But now in Christ Jesus you who sometimes were far off are made nigh by the blood of Christ"* (Eph. 2:13).

"Much more then, being now justified by His blood, we shall be saved from wrath through Him" (Rom. 5:9).

Jesus said that the New Testament or new covenant is *"in My blood"* (I Cor. 11:25).

The blood alone is the token, and if anyone tries to put anything else as a token, he has just abrogated God's plan of salvation and will bring upon himself utter, spiritual ruin.

THE PLAGUE

Whatever the plague was, it would take the lives of the firstborn of both man and beast. It was a type of sin, which destroys.

The only remedy for sin is the *"shed blood of the Lamb,"* i.e., the Cross.

It is the blood of Christ that gives peace, imparts perfect justification—divine righteousness—purges the conscience, brings us into the holiest of all, justifies God in receiving the believing sinner, and constitutes our title to all the joys, the dignities, and the glories of heaven (Rom. 3:24-26; 5:9; Eph. 2:13-18; Col. 1:20-22; Heb. 9:14; 10:19; I Pet. 1:19; 2:24; I Jn. 1:7; Rev. 7:14-17; 12:11).

One preacher of the Word of Faith doctrine made the statement that the blood of Jesus alone would not effect redemption. His reasoning was that scores of other people died on crosses that day, and their blood did not effect any redemption.

THE BLOOD OF JESUS

Such thinking proves a serious lack of knowledge of the Word of God. Of course, the shed blood of the other individuals who died on crosses that day did not effect redemption because it could not effect redemption. The blood of Jesus effected redemption and brought about the possibility of the changed life, i.e., the born-again experience, simply because of who Jesus is, and what Jesus is.

All others who died that day were sinners; therefore, their blood was polluted, tainted, ill-affected, etc. Consequently, God could not accept any of them as He could not accept any man.

In fact, God would have to become man, which He did, keep the law perfectly, and then pay its penalty on the Cross, which He did by the sacrifice of Himself (Gal. 1:4).

Only God could do this great thing, and He could do it only in the form of a man. It had to be this way because it was not angels who were being redeemed, and it certainly wasn't members of the Godhead being redeemed, but rather man— the entirety of mankind—at least for all who will believe. So, God would have to become a man, which He did.

Jesus Christ was perfect in every respect; therefore, God could accept His poured out life, of which the blood was a token, as payment for the terrible sin question.

WHY BLOOD?

We have addressed this already but suffice to say, the life of the flesh is in the blood. So, when the blood is poured out, this means the life is given, which is what Christ did.

It was not so much that the blood within itself had some magical effect, and neither did it mean that it being shed had some magical effect.

Rather, it refers to the life of Christ being given, which paid the price.

At the same time, His life had to be given in the form of the shedding of His blood.

However, it was absolutely imperative that that life be perfect in every respect, and that His physical body also be perfect in every respect. Otherwise, it could not be accepted. That's the reason that He could not be stoned to death or killed in any other manner; it had to be on a Cross.

WHY THE CROSS?

When Jesus paid the price, it was a price that included every single sin, irrespective of how bad it was. In other words, He atoned for all sin (I Jn. 1:7).

In the Old Testament economy, when an Israelite committed a dastardly crime, he was first stoned to death, and then his body was placed on a tree for several hours, actually, till sundown to show that he was cursed by God. It was not to remain on the tree all night but was to be taken down before sundown and then buried.

Paul would refer to this by saying: *"Christ has redeemed us from the curse of the law, being made a curse for us: for it is written, Cursed is everyone who hangs on a tree"* (Gal. 3:13).

In fact, and as stated, Jesus had to die on a Cross; however, it should be understood that He really wasn't cursed by God, but was rather *"made a curse,"* which is far different than being cursed. Sin causes one to be cursed by God. Jesus had never sinned, so He could not be cursed by God, but He could be made a curse. This simply refers to the fact of bearing the penalty of sin, which is death.

WITHOUT THE SHEDDING OF BLOOD

While on the Cross, He poured out His life's blood through the many wounds on His body that, in effect, poured out His life, which atoned for all sin, at least for those who will believe (Jn. 3:16). Without the shedding of blood, there is no remission of sin (Heb. 9:22).

Once again, we emphasize the fact that it had to be the blood of Christ; it could be no other. His blood alone would suffice because it was untouched by the fall in the garden of Eden. In fact, that's the reason that Jesus had to be born of a virgin. To have been born otherwise, that is, as man is normally born, would have inculcated upon Himself the results of the fall, which would have meant that He would have been born in sin as all other men. Due to the fact that He was born of the Virgin Mary, which means that He was not procreated by man, it means that He was born without original sin.

THE PLAGUE OF SIN

As we have repeatedly stated, it was only Christ in His sacrificial atoning death that could address the terrible problem of sin. It cannot be addressed by education, money, motivation, good deeds, or, in fact, anything that man does. Its power is beyond the ability of man. That's what makes it so foolish as it regards the church stooping to man's ways—we refer to humanistic psychology—to address this terrible monster. It can be addressed only by the Cross, and the Cross alone!

The explanation that I have just given regarding Chapter 12 of Exodus is crystal clear. It could not be any clearer than what is portrayed here and, in fact, the entirety of the Bible.

Sin destroys everything it touches, and the only answer for sin is the Cross, i.e., the shed blood of Christ.

SATAN AND THE CROSS

That's the reason that Satan will do everything within his power to push the church away from the Cross. He really doesn't care too very much about whatever direction the church takes, just as long as it's away from the Cross.

That's why Paul preached the Cross so strongly. When the Lord explained to him the meaning of the new covenant, which was the meaning of the Cross (Gal. 1:11-12), he then knew that the only answer for man's dilemma was the Cross of Christ (Gal. 6:14).

That's the reason the Judaizers were so wrong in Paul's day; they were pulling people away from the Cross. That's the reason the modern Word of Faith doctrine is so wrong; it pulls people away from the Cross. That's the reason humanistic psychology and its devotees are so wrong; it pulls people away from the Cross.

A FEAST TO THE LORD

"And this day shall be unto you for a memorial; and you shall keep it a feast to the LORD throughout your generations; you shall keep it a feast by an ordinance forever" (Ex. 12:14).

Actually, when one accepts Christ, one, in effect, at least

in the mind of God, is keeping the Passover.

Paul also stated:

> *Purge out therefore the old leaven* (spoken in old covenant terminology, but with the same meaning carried over in the hearts and lives of New Testament believers), *that you may be a new lump* (start acting like what you are, 'a new creation'), *as you are unleavened* (speaks of the position that one has in Christ; that is our 'standing'; it is the business of the Spirit to bring our 'state' up to our 'standing'). *For even Christ our Passover is sacrificed for us* (the believer can have victory over the sin nature by placing his faith exclusively in the Cross of Christ, which sacrifice addressed all sin): *therefore let us keep the Feast* (is meant to serve as a symbol of the Jewish Passover, when all leaven was purged from the household), *not with old leaven* (old sins committed before conversion), *neither with the leaven of malice and wickedness* (refers to the ways of the world from which the child of God has been delivered); *but with the unleavened bread of sincerity and truth* (can only be attained by one's faith being anchored solely in the sacrifice of Christ) (I Cor. 5:7-8).

ALL OLD TESTAMENT TYPES AND SHADOWS WERE SATISFIED IN CHRIST

Let us say it again: Everything in the Old Testament

economy, so to speak, pointed to Christ. So, when one accepts Christ, one fully keeps all that the old law contained. In other words, when one accepts Christ, the Passover is automatically kept in Him. As well, the Great Day of Atonement becomes an every day of the atonement. So, it is foolish for a modern believer to try to keep the Passover, any of the feast days of the law of Moses, or anything from that time frame because Christ has satisfied it all. When one accepts Christ, one is then fully compliant with all that the law demanded.

A MEMORIAL

The Passover was required to be kept on the fourteenth of Abib each and every year, *"throughout your generations."* The Scripture says in this verse that it is to be done forever.

Let us say it again: When one accepts Christ as one's Saviour and Lord, all of these things are automatically kept. The Scripture says, *"For Christ is the end of the law for righteousness to everyone who believes"* (Rom. 10:4).

After the great event of the Cross, it is not God's will for men to continue to look to the "types" when, in fact, the "antitype" has come and has fulfilled all the types. Why does one want to offer up the sacrifices of animals when the sacrifice has been offered!

In fact, this was a terrible problem for the Christian Jews in the early church. They kept trying to keep the law as well as serve Christ. It caused the Apostle Paul great problems, with these individuals attempting to continue the Old Testament practices when, in fact, Christ and what He did for us at the Cross is our Passover (I Cor. 5:7).

FOREVER

The question might well be asked as to the meaning of the word *forever* as it is used here. In the perfect age to come, which is graphically outlined in Revelation, Chapters 21 and 22, the word *Lamb*, as it refers to Christ, is used seven times. Now, please understand, in this perfect age to come, Satan and all his minions of darkness, plus every unsaved soul, will be in the lake of fire. To be sure, they will be there forever. There will be no more sin or transgression of any nature, but yet, as stated, the Holy Spirit refers seven times to the "Lamb." So, I think that this tells us that in some fashion, this "memorial" will be kept forever.

The word *Lamb*, referring to Christ, is used in this fashion, I think, in order that all believers may know and understand that the great and glorious privileges that we will have forever and forever are all brought about as a result of what Jesus did at the Cross. Those privileges include the New Jerusalem coming down from God out of heaven, with God literally transferring His headquarters from heaven to earth.

That's at least one of the reasons that the Cross of Christ must be the central theme of the gospel. In fact, there is no salvation, no victory, and no grace of God outside of the Cross. If we preach anything else, we're preaching a false gospel, and the Apostle Paul said, *"Let him be accursed"* (Gal. 1:8-9).

AN ILLUSTRATION

Why is it that the church ignores the Cross when, in reality, its theme is so abundantly presented in the entirety of the Word of God? Why do we insist upon promoting other means of life and victory when, in fact, there are no other means? That's why Paul was so adamant as it regarded this gospel message. The truth is, and the facts are, the gospel is the Cross, and the Cross is the gospel (I Cor. 1:17-18, 21, 23; 2:2, 5).

A short time ago, a Charismatic leader had a severe spiritual problem, in other words, a bondage of a severe nature. It was found out and, regrettably and sadly, the church took its usual course.

The following is the solution they presented for his problem, which pretty well mirrors the so-called solution of most of the modern church presently.

It consisted somewhat of the following:

- He was not to preach for three months.

- He was to place himself under the authority of two particular preachers, one, if I remember correctly, who lived in Europe, and another who lived at least 1,000 miles from him.

- He was to undergo an extensive period of counseling from a psychologist.

Now, that was the solution that the church presented, which completely ignored and, in fact, repudiated the Cross.

In the first place, how in the world does preaching or not preaching affect the bondage that grips this man? What in the world does not preaching for three months have to do with his deliverance?

THE CROSS OF CHRIST IS THE ONLY ANSWER FOR SIN

What in the world can two preachers do for anyone as it regards a bondage? His calling them everyday and talking with them over the phone will effect no answer for his dilemma.

Then, the crowning insult of all is the turning to Egypt for relief, i.e., the psychologist.

What do you, the reader, think that psychologists actually do? I can tell you very easily what they do.

They just talk to the individual. They don't have a miracle drug they can give him or her in order for the problem to be solved. They can only talk.

Now, let me make another statement: If this terrible problem of sin could be talked away, then Jesus needlessly came down here and died on a Cross (Gal. 2:20-21).

The truth is, this brother can engage in these particular pursuits as long as he desires and with great dedication, and he'll be the same man when he comes out as when he went in. This means that if he doesn't come to the Cross, his life and ministry are wrecked and ruined. There is no way that victory can be his in such a capacity.

In the first place, sin is so awful, so terrible, and so powerful that there is no way that it can be addressed, at least properly, other than faith exercised in Christ and what He has done for us at the Cross.

When this is done, the Holy Spirit comes in and performs His great and glorious work, which guarantees victory.

BIBLICAL RESTORATION

It's a shame, but the far greater majority of the modern church doesn't have the slightest idea of the meaning of biblical restoration; consequently, there is precious little scriptural restoration in its ranks, or restoration of any kind for that matter. What does the Bible teach as it regards this subject?

Paul said, *"Brethren, if a man be overtaken in a fault* (a moral failure), *you who are spiritual, restore such an one in the spirit of meekness; considering yourself, lest you also be tempted"* (Gal. 6:1).

The key to this is the word *spiritual.* It refers to one who walks after the Spirit (Rom. 8:1-2).

A spiritual man or woman is one who understands that everything we have in Christ comes to us because of what He did for us at the Cross.

He places his faith in that finished work and maintains his faith in that finished work; consequently, the Holy Spirit works grandly within his heart and life (Jn. 7:37-39; 16:7-14).

One who is spiritual is one who understands the Cross of Christ relative to our sanctification. Therefore, if a person fails the Lord, irrespective of what the failure might be, one who is spiritual is to tell such a person why he failed.

And why did he fail?

FAILURE

All failure can be attributed to faith that is taken from the Cross of Christ and, in fact, placed in something else. Such a position guarantees failure. There is only one victory over sin.

Paul graphically explained it to us. He said, *"For the law of the Spirit of life in Christ Jesus has made me free from the law of sin and death"* (Rom. 8:2).

This *"law of the Spirit of life in Christ Jesus"* refers to the manner and the way in which the Holy Spirit works. The short phrase, *"in Christ Jesus,"* proclaims the basis on which He works.

It refers to what Jesus did on the Cross, which demands faith on our part.

So, the spiritual one is to explain to the one who has failed the Lord that he failed simply because his faith was placed in things other than Christ and the Cross. This, in effect, at least in the eyes of God, makes him (or her) a spiritual adulterer (Rom. 7:1-4).

Of course, as we have repeatedly stated, the Holy Spirit is not going to have anything to do with such a position.

He honors faith in Christ and the Cross, and faith in Christ and the Cross alone.

The spiritual one is to get the person's faith back in the Cross, which means it is now exclusively in Christ and what He has done for us, and that person will once again begin to walk in victory. That is biblical restoration. Anything else is outside of the scope of the Word of God and is guaranteed to bring no positive results.

That's the reason that Paul also said in Chapter 6 of Galatians: *"But God forbid that I should glory (boast), save in the Cross of our Lord Jesus Christ, by whom the world is crucified unto me, and I unto the world"* (Gal. 6:14).

WILLPOWER

Most Christians have the erroneous idea that when they give their heart to Christ, He gives them greater willpower. He doesn't! The will of the believer is the same as it was before his or her conversion. While the will is definitely important—*"whosoever will"*—within itself, it's not enough.

If that's what it takes to overcome sin, then Jesus didn't need to come down here and die on a Cross.

Now, what I'm about to say is going to be strong, but it is true.

Satan can override the will of a believer and make that believer do things that he or she doesn't want to do. In fact, such is happening millions of times each and every day all over the world.

Let's say it this way: If the believer is trying to overcome sin by the strength of his or her will, this means that he isn't looking to Christ and the Cross, but rather to self. Such a believer will fail every single time, no matter how hard he tries to do otherwise. Tragically, that's where most modern believers are. Most have absolutely no knowledge whatsoever of the part the Cross of Christ plays in their everyday life and living for God. They understand the Cross relative to salvation, but then, that's where their understanding ceases.

The fact is, virtually all of Paul's writings in his 14 epistles pertain to the believer living for God.

The great apostle took a page from his own life and living after he was saved, filled with the Spirit, and was preaching the gospel. But yet, by not knowing God's prescribed order of victory, he was living a life of spiritual failure. In fact, it was to Paul that this great truth was given (Gal. 1:1-12). This is what the apostle said about willpower:

"For I know that in me (that is, in my flesh,) *dwells no good thing: for to will is present with me* (there is the willpower); *but how to perform that which is good I find not"* (Rom. 7:18).

In this passage, he plainly tells us that the will within itself is not strong enough to overcome sin. Now, we must understand that when Paul wrote this, he full well knew and understood God's prescribed order of victory, which is the Cross. However, for a period of several years, he did not know and struggled, exactly as Chapter 7 of Romans brings out. No, the answer is not a super willpower, but rather the

Cross of Christ, and the Cross of Christ alone.

IGNORANCE OR UNBELIEF?

The Message of the Cross is by no means new but is that which was preached and taught by the Apostle Paul. When the Lord began to open up this great truth of the Cross to me in 1997, I at first thought that the reason the church had so gone astray was because of scriptural ignorance as it regarded this all important subject. Of course, that was true in many cases; however, I have come to see, I think, that the majority of the cases don't fall into the category of ignorance, but rather of unbelief.

In other words, most of the modern church, preachers included, simply don't believe that what Jesus did at the Cross is the answer to hurting, sick, ailing, and sinning humanity. They rather resort to the wisdom of men, which, in effect, is no wisdom at all.

Unbelief is a deadly thing. It is perhaps the basis of all sin and the result of all sin. In fact, this is the first work of the Holy Spirit.

Jesus said:

"Nevertheless I tell you the truth; It is expedient for you that I go away: for if I go not away, the Comforter will not come unto you; but if I depart, I will send Him unto you. And when He is come, He will reprove (convict) the world of sin, and of righteousness, and of judgment: of sin, because they believe not on Me" (Jn. 16:7-9).

SIN AND THE CROSS

The only answer for sin in any form is the Cross of Christ. We must remember that, never forget that, and ever understand that. If anything else is promoted, we sin, and we sin greatly.

So, preachers who are promoting means and ways other than the Cross are not only promoting something that is of no value but, as well, whether they realize it or not, are insulting Christ greatly. In essence, to promote anything other than the Cross of Christ as the answer to man's dilemma is, in effect, saying that what Jesus did at the Cross is not enough, and we have to add our efforts to His.

If one is to notice that which is presently happening, when that road is taken, after a little while, the Cross of Christ becomes less and less, with man's foolish ways more and more, until finally, the Cross is out of the picture altogether. That's exactly what has happened and is happening to the modern church.

Anything other than Christ and the Cross presents rebellion against the plan of God, and nothing could be worse than that.

That's why Paul said, and rightly so:

I marvel that you are so soon removed from Him (the Holy Spirit) *who called you into the grace of Christ* (made possible by the Cross) *unto another gospel* (anything which doesn't have the Cross as its object of faith):

Which is not another (presents the fact that Satan's aim is not so much to deny the Gospel, which he can little do, as to corrupt it); *but there be some who trouble you, and would pervert the Gospel of Christ* (once again, to make the object of faith something other than the Cross).

But though we (Paul and his associates), *or an angel from heaven, preach any other gospel unto you than that which we have preached unto you* (Jesus Christ and Him crucified), *let him be accursed* (eternally condemned; the Holy Spirit speaks this through Paul, making this very serious) (Gal. 1:6-8).

THE FEAST OF UNLEAVENED BREAD

Seven days shall you eat unleavened bread; even the first day you shall put away leaven out of your houses: for whosoever eats leavened bread from the first day until the seventh day, that soul shall be cut off from Israel.

And in the first day there shall be an holy convocation, and in the seventh day there shall be an holy convocation to you; no manner of work shall be done in them, save that which every man must eat, that only may be done of you.

And you shall observe the feast of unleavened bread; for in this selfsame day have I brought your armies out of the land of Egypt: therefore shall you observe this day in your generations by an ordinance forever.

In the first month, on the fourteenth day of the month at evening, you shall eat unleavened bread, until the one and twentieth day of the month at evening.

Seven days shall there be no leaven found in your houses: for whosoever eats that which is leavened, even that soul shall be cut off from the congregation of Israel, whether he be a stranger, or born in the land.

You shall eat nothing leavened; in all your habitations shall you eat unleavened bread" (Ex. 12:15-20).

THE PASSOVER FEAST

The Feast of Unleavened Bread was to be kept in conjunction with the Passover Feast. Of course, Jesus fulfilled this which is given here just as He did the Passover; however, the great truths contained therein are minutely significant for us presently.

What did it all mean?

The unleavened bread, first of all, typified Christ as it regarded His perfect life, free from all sin and contamination. Leaven is yeast, which brings about rot and fermentation.

In the Old Testament, even as here, it is used as a type of sin and evil.

Jesus would have no sin and no evil and was the fulfillment of the Feast of Unleavened Bread.

The believer is to live accordingly as his Master. There is to be no sin within our lives. This doesn't refer to sinless perfection because the Bible doesn't teach such, but it does refer to the fact that sin must not have dominion over us in any way (Rom. 6:14).

As long as we live in this physical body, which is not yet redeemed, there will be, at times, evil thoughts or even evil acts, which constitute sin.

However, that is a far cry from sin dominating the person in some way. The Feast of Unleavened Bread proclaims the fact that such is not to be.

As stated, the Scripture plainly states, *"Sin shall not have dominion over you"* (Rom. 6:14).

THE NUMBER SEVEN

As we have repeatedly stated, the only way this type of life can be lived, and I mean the only way, is by the believer understanding that all things come to him from God due to what Christ did at the Cross. His faith is to be anchored completely in the Cross, and the Cross alone, which, in effect, refers to what Jesus there did, and then the Holy Spirit will work mightily on his behalf (Rom. 6:3-5, 11).

The Feast of Unleavened Bread was to last for seven days. The number seven denotes God's number of perfection, completion, universality, and totality.

So, in essence, the meaning of the number seven, as it is given here, refers to the fact that the entirety of our lives in totality is to be a Feast of Unleavened Bread, so to speak.

In other words, victorious living is to be ours seven days a week, 52 weeks of the year, for the entirety of our existence on this earth.

The believer was to *"put away leaven out of your* (their) *houses"* (Ex. 12:15). This corresponds with the words of Paul: *"I beseech you therefore, brethren, by the mercies of God, that you present your bodies a living sacrifice, holy, acceptable unto God, which is your reasonable service"* (Rom. 12:1).

THE MESSAGE OF THE CROSS

Paul also said: *"Wherefore seeing we also are compassed about with so great a cloud of witnesses, let us lay aside every weight, and the sin which does so easily beset us, and let us run with patience the race that is set before us"* (Heb. 12:1).

Now the great question is, how is the believer to do this?

The amazing thing about the Message of the Cross is that it applies itself to every facet of our lives and living.

In fact, the believer can do this only in one way: As stated over and over, the believer is to place his faith in the sacrifice of Christ and realize that this is the only manner in which we can overcome the world (Gal. 6:14). The Holy Spirit is the One who must do these things for us, and through the Holy

Spirit alone can it be done. He works exclusively within the parameters of the finished work of Christ (Jn. 14:16-18; 16:7-14). He demands only that our faith ever be in that finished work.

THE LORD SAVES US FROM SIN, NOT IN SIN

The Scripture plainly tells us that if the believer in Old Testament times ignored this feast, his soul would be cut off from Israel, meaning that he would be eternally lost (Ex. 12:15).

Paul said this same thing, as well, when he listed the *"works of the flesh"* and then said, *"Of the which I tell you before, as I have also told you in time past, that they which do such things shall not inherit the kingdom of God"* (Gal. 5:19-21).

The Lord saves us from sin, not in sin. The idea that we can continue to allow sin to dominate us in any fashion, considering the price that Christ paid on the Cross, is a perversion of the Word of God.

Domination of sin will harden the heart. Such will always ultimately bring on unbelief.

While the Lord will never throw over a believer because of sin—even the vilest of sin—the believer can definitely cease to believe, thereby, becoming an unbeliever and, thus, be eternally lost.

The key to accepting Christ and serving Christ is faith. If faith in Christ is lost, the soul will be lost as well.

To be sure, sin domination definitely can bring on unbelief and, in fact, will bring on unbelief if allowed to continue. However, it doesn't have to continue because victory can be ours in every capacity if we will only make the finished work of Christ the object of our faith.

FAITH AND WORKS

Verse 16 tells us, *"No manner of work shall be done in them,"* referring to these particular seven days. This foreshadows the fact that salvation and victory are not of works, but rather of faith.

Listen again to Paul: *"For in Jesus Christ neither circumcision avails anything, nor uncircumcision; but faith which works by love"* (Gal. 5:6).

It is all by faith and not at all by works (Eph. 2:8-9).

When we say faith, without exception, we are always speaking of faith in Christ and what Christ has done for us at the Cross. Christ and His work must never be divided or separated in any manner. It is always, even as Paul said, *"We preach Christ crucified"* (I Cor. 1:23).

A HOLY CONVOCATION

The Feast of Unleavened Bread was to be a *"holy convocation,"* which referred to a gathering together and all participating. Later on, when safely ensconced in the land of Israel, this would be carried out literally, with a male from each household attending the feast at Jerusalem. It could only be carried out symbolically in Egypt, which would be obvious. It corresponds to the fact that all of this was very important in the eyes of God and had to be subscribed to without fail. Our church services should be the express purpose of preaching the Cross. It must be preached in order for sinners to be saved; it must be preached in order for Christians to live victoriously. There is no other way!

The Feast of Unleavened Bread was meant to celebrate the deliverance of the children of Israel from Egyptian bondage. We are to boast in the Cross because it has delivered us through Christ from the world, the flesh, and the Devil (Gal. 6:14).

AN EVERLASTING COVENANT

"It is to be observed in your generations by an ordinance forever" (Ex. 12:17).

Paul referred to what Jesus did as *"an everlasting covenant"* (Heb. 13:20). The Cross, which is the fulfillment of why Christ came, who was perfect in every respect and, thereby, the perfect sacrifice, is to be celebrated forever.

The phrase, *"In the first month,"* as it regards Verse 18, refers to the fact that Christ and His Cross are to be first and foremost.

While the Cross can be referred to as a doctrine, still, the truth is, every Bible doctrine must be built on the foundation of the Cross, or else, it will be specious in some way.

The phrase, *"Whether he be a stranger, or born in the land,"* of Verse 19 proclaims the fact that Jesus and Him crucified is the answer for the entirety of the world. Verse 20 says, *"You shall eat nothing leavened,"* meaning that God cannot accept sin in any form. Christ is to never be associated with sin, except in the respect of taking it away (Jn. 1:29).

THE COMMAND

"Then Moses called for all the elders of Israel, and said unto them, Draw out and take you a lamb according to your families, and kill the passover" (Ex. 12:21).

The Passover and the Feast of Unleavened Bread began at the same time, the 15th day of Abib, or as it was later called, Nisan, which would be sometime after sundown on the 14TH.

The blood was to be applied to the doorposts of the houses with hyssop. It speaks not of Christ, but of the sinner's appropriation of His sacrifice.

And when He sees the blood—not our good works, not our church membership, not our social contacts, not our wealth, and not our education, but the blood, the blood of Christ, at that—He will keep back the destroyer.

CONCERNING THE PASSOVER

Pink says:

The institution and ritual of the Passover supply us with one of the most striking and blessed foreshadowments of the Cross work of Christ to be found anywhere in the Old Testament. Its importance may be gathered from the frequency with which the title of 'Lamb' is afterwards applied to the Saviour, a title which looks back to what is before us in Exodus, Chapter 12.

Messianic prediction contemplated the suffering Messiah, 'brought as a Lamb to the slaughter' (Isa. 53:7). John the Baptist hailed Him as 'Behold the Lamb of God which takes away the sin of the world' (Jn. 1:29). The apostle speaks of Him as 'a Lamb without blemish and without spot (I Pet. 1:19).

While the one who leaned on the Master's bosom employs this title no less than twenty-eight times in the closing book of Scripture, thus, an Old Testament prophet, the Lord's forerunner, an apostle, and the apocalyptic seer unite in employing this term 'Lamb' of the Redeemer.

Throughout the entirety of the Old Testament, we find pictures and portrayals of the sacrificial work of Christ. However, Chapter 12 of Exodus, I think, supplies the grandest picture of all in the prefiguring account.

THE GOD-WARD AND MAN-WARD ASPECTS OF THE ATONEMENT

The Passover portrays to us and, in fact, sets before us the

God-ward and the man-ward aspects of the atonement. It portrays Christ satisfying the demands of deity as it regards the righteousness, holiness, and justice of God, while, at the same time, it views Christ as a substitute for believing sinners. There is hardly any picture of the Cross that is not supplied in the account given in Chapter 12.

As stated, the Passover and the Feast of Unleavened Bread were to begin at the same time, which was the 14TH day of Abib, which somewhat corresponds with our April. The blood was to then be applied to the doorposts, with the Feast of Unleavened Bread then beginning, and concluding on the 21ST day of the month. More than likely, the deliverance was effected the night of the 21ST, or at the latest, the 22ND.

THE LAMB TO BE KILLED

Each family was to kill a lamb, unless the family was too small to do such. With that being the case, they would join with the family next door, but the fact was, all were to kill the lamb. It was not that every particular individual—man, woman, and child—shared in the act itself, but that they did so representatively. The head of the household stood for and acted on behalf of each member of his family.

All are guilty of sin and worthy of judgment; consequently, all who respect Christ as the true Paschal Lamb can have absolute and conscious redemption from all sin. As a result, there will be a consequent separation from and deliverance out of this present evil world.

The lamb was to be killed, typifying Christ and the death He would suffer on the Cross, which was necessary in order for man to be redeemed. That's why Paul said, *"We preach Christ crucified"* (I Cor. 1:23).

The church presently, at least for the most part, is serving *"another Jesus"* (II Cor. 11:4).

By that I refer to a Jesus other than the Jesus of the Cross. Let it ever be understood that if the Cross ever ceases to be the center of emphasis, then, pure and simple, it is another Jesus whom man is serving.

PAUL

Paul is the man to whom the meaning of the new covenant was given, which, in effect, is the meaning of the Cross. That's the reason that he so solemnly preached the Cross (I Cor. 1:23). He knew that if anything else was preached, it would bring destruction on the ones who heeded the false message. Regrettably, at the present time, almost all that comes from behind modern pulpits can be deduced as none other than false.

There is one thing for certain: The message presently being preached is not "Jesus Christ and Him crucified." So, where does that leave the people?

That leaves the people without the blood applied to the doorposts, i.e., the heart. You can draw your own conclusions thereafter.

Again I state, this is the reason that Paul wrote his epistle to the Galatians in the manner in which he did. In fact, he was angry when this epistle was written. By that, I speak of righteous indignation.

ANOTHER GOSPEL

The Galatians had been brought to Christ under Paul's ministry, or else, those who were associated with him; consequently, they were brought in correctly.

However, after Paul left and went to other fields of endeavor, false teachers came in and attempted to promote the doctrine of works by linking such with grace. In other words, they were saying that while Jesus must be accepted, as well, the law of Moses must be kept. Paul called that "another gospel," which, in effect, was no gospel at all (Gal. 1:6-7).

He knew this false message would save no sinners and give no victory to Christians. Therefore, he would further say: *"But though we, or an angel from heaven, preach any other gospel unto you than that which we have preached unto you* (Jesus Christ and Him crucified), *let him be accursed"* (Gal. 1:8).

I think it should go without saying that these are strong words. In fact, what the apostle says here places every single preacher in the world on one side or the other. In other words, they are preaching the Cross, or they aren't preaching the Cross.

So, let me ask the reader, How many preachers with which you are acquainted are presently preaching the Cross?

HYSSOP

"And you shall take a bunch of hyssop, and dip it in the blood that is in the bason, and strike the lintel and the two side posts with the blood that is in the bason; and none of you shall go out at the door of his house until the morning" (Ex. 12:22).

The hyssop was not connected with the lamb, but with the application of its blood. It speaks then not of Christ, but of the sinner's appropriation of the sacrifice of Christ.

The hyssop is never found in connection with any of the offerings that foreshadowed the Lord Jesus Himself. It is beheld, uniformly, in the hands of the sinner. Thus, in connection with the cleansing of the leper (Lev., Chpt. 14) and the restoration of the unclean (Num., Chpt. 19), we find the application, as well, of the word *hyssop.*

From Psalm 51:7, we may learn that hyssop speaks of "humiliation of soul, contrition, and repentance."

Note that in I Kings 4:33, hyssop is contrasted with the cedars, showing that hyssop speaks of lowliness.

Incidentally, hyssop was a type of grass that grew in crevices between the rocks.

THE BLOOD

The word *bason* is not exactly the best translation. It should read, *"With the blood that is* on the threshold."

The idea is that the lamb was killed in front of each house, or at least somewhere close to the house, which, in effect, served as the "threshold," or the place where the house was entered, i.e., the door. However, when the actual blood was applied, it was to be applied only on the side posts and the header.

Whenever the people went into their houses at night, and this was after the blood was applied, they were to remain in the house all night and not go out until the next morning.

This tells us that the death angel was to come through at night, and beyond the protection of the blood of the lamb, there was no assurance of safety. In fact, there was no safety outside of this application, just as there is no safety presently outside of this application, i.e., the blood.

THE CROSS

We are to never regard the Cross of Christ as a mere circumstance in the life of Christ, referring to His sin-bearing. It was the grand and only scene of sin-bearing.

Peter said, *"His own self bear our sins in His own body on the tree"* (I Pet. 2:24).

He did not bear our sins anywhere else. He did not bear them in the manger, in the wilderness, or in the garden, but *"only on the tree."* In fact, He never had aught to say to sin, save on the Cross; and there He bowed His head and yielded up His precious life under the accumulated weight of His people's sins. Neither did He ever suffer at the hand of God, save on the Cross, and there Jehovah hid His face from Him because He was made to be sin (II Cor. 5:21).

In contemplating the Cross, we find in it that which cancels all our guilt. This imparts sweet peace and joy. However, we find in it also the complete setting aside of nature—the crucifixion of the flesh—the death of the *"old man"* (Rom. 6:6; Gal. 2:20; 6:14; Col. 2:11).

THE DESTROYER

"For the LORD *will pass through to smite the Egyptians; and when He sees the blood upon the lintel* (header), *and on the two side posts, the* LORD *will pass over the door, and will not suffer the destroyer to come in unto your houses to smite you"* (Ex. 12:23).

The Hebrew word for destroyer is *shachath* and means "to decay, ruin, cast off, perish, waste, destroy."

It has been debated as to whether the Lord was referring to Himself as a destroyer, or rather a destroying angel, or even the death angel.

I think it can be safely said that the Lord is speaking here not of Himself but of a destroying angel. When the Lord speaks of doing things, and puts Himself in the position as the actual participant, such doesn't necessarily mean that He personally carries out whatever it is that's being done. He is said to have done certain things when, in fact, He would use agents to carry out that which He desired. However, the fact is, they—whether angels, men, or even Satan—can only do what our Lord bids be done.

FACING THE DESTROYER

There is another lesson here that is even of far greater significance than that which we have just addressed. It concerns the fact that anyone who stands in the way of the plan of God or the people of God will ultimately face the destroyer. With the children of Israel serving as slaves in Egypt, and that nation being possibly the most powerful on earth, it serves as a perfect example. It doesn't really matter how seemingly weak God's way may seem to be or how strong the opposing forces seem to be, the actual truth is the opposite.

The Scripture says: *"If God be for us, who can be against us?"* (Rom. 8:31). Nothing is stronger than God, which should be obvious. So, all who oppose Him will ultimately face the destroyer. All should heed carefully those words.

THE BLOOD

Again, let it be emphasized that the only thing, and we mean the only thing, that stood between the children of Israel and the destroyer was the blood. It is no less the same at the present. It is the blood alone that protects the individual. That's why the Lord said: *"When I see the blood, I will pass over you, and the plague shall not be upon you to destroy you"* (Ex. 12:13).

Of course, when we speak of the blood, we are at the same time speaking of the Cross. In fact, the Cross is a synonym for the death, burial, resurrection, ascension, and exaltation of the Lord Jesus Christ. In other words, it incorporates all that He did for lost humanity in regard to the price that He paid; however, of these things we have just named, it was the Cross where the price was actually paid. All the other things, the resurrection, the ascension, and exaltation, are predicated solely on the fact of the Cross. It was on the Cross where Jesus shed His blood and poured out His life as a sacrifice, which atoned for all sin—past, present, and future—at least for those who will believe (Jn. 3:16).

BOASTING!

This means that as important as was our Lord's virgin birth, His perfect life, His miracles, etc., none of that redeemed lost humanity. Had His life and mission stopped there, not one single soul would have been saved. It took the Cross to bring about heaven's redemption plan.

That's why Paul, under the inspiration of the Holy Spirit, said, *"But God forbid that I should glory* (boast), *save in the Cross of our Lord Jesus Christ"* (Gal. 6:14).

That's why he also said, *"For Christ sent me not to baptize, but to preach the gospel: not with wisdom of words, lest the Cross of Christ should be made of none effect"* (I Cor. 1:17).

It grieves me to no end when I see Christians, even preachers, who are in deep trouble, yet they place their faith in the silly rules either made up by men, or ones they have concocted themselves, which means that they are throwing over the Cross. They may deny this; however, one cannot have it both ways. One is either trusting Christ and what He did for us at the Cross, or one is trusting other things, and the two can never mix.

In the first place, the work of Christ on the Cross was and is a finished work (Heb. 1:2-3).

FOREVER

"And you shall observe this thing for an ordinance to you and to your sons forever" (Ex. 12:24).

Some three times the Lord ordered Israel to keep the Feast of the Passover forever (Ex. 12:14, 17, 24), and implied it in Exodus 13:10.

In essence, this tells us that the work of Christ on the Cross was and is a finished work, which means that it will never have to be repeated, and there will never have to be anything added.

In fact, under the old covenant, which Moses would receive from the Lord very shortly, the duties of the priests were never finished; consequently, while there were many other items of sacred vessels, utensils, and furniture in the tabernacle and temple, there was no chair. The work had to keep going constantly simply because the blood of bulls and goats could not take away sins (Heb. 10:4). Actually, the very meaning of the crucifixion is that it was a work that was accomplished in time past and will never have to be repeated, with its blessings continuing forever. In fact, it will never be discontinued.

This is why we sin greatly when we ignore the Cross, or else, we try to add to the Cross. Such constitutes grievous sins, with Paul even referring to such people as *"enemies of the Cross"* (Phil. 3:18-19).

The Cross was the plan of God formed before the foundation of the world (I Pet. 1:18-20), it is the plan of God now, and it will continue to be the plan of God forever. There is nothing else coming because there is nothing else needed.

THE PROMISE

"And it shall come to pass, when you be come to the land which the LORD will give you, according as He has promised, that you shall keep this service" (Ex. 12:25).

Every promise of God, without exception, is based on the great sacrifice of Christ. Now, that's quite a statement and needs to be enlarged upon.

The central core of the plan of God is the sacrifice of Christ. The central core of that sacrifice is the blood.

However, it's not just any blood, but rather the blood of a divinely appointed victim. That victim is the Lord Jesus Christ. As well, this divinely appointed victim was spotless as it referred to His life, which means that He was *"holy, harmless, undefiled, separate from sinners"* (Heb. 7:26).

Furthermore, His blood atoned for all sin—past, present, and future; however, it is only for those who will believe (Jn. 3:16).

And most important of all, faith in the shed blood of Christ can save the soul, and it alone can save the soul (I Pet. 1:18-20).

Let us once again say, even as we've already said many times, the Cross of Christ is not only the center of circumference, so to speak, for the salvation of the soul but, as well, for the sanctification of the saint (Rom. 6:3-5, 11, 14; 8:1-2, 11).

God had promised the children of Israel the Promised Land. It was based entirely upon the sacrifice of Christ.

How was this so?

THE SACRIFICE OF CHRIST?

Despite the children of Israel being a chosen people, even raised up specifically by the Lord for an expressed purpose, still, they were sinful people. Due to that sin, God could not deal with them directly but had to do so through intermediaries, and I speak of the priests, but most of all, the sacrificial system. It was the duty of the priests to faithfully carry out the commands of the Lord as it regarded this particular system. Through the sacrificial system, God could have a modicum of fellowship and rapport with His people. While animal blood could not take away sin, it did serve as a temporary atonement until Christ would come, to which every animal sacrifice always pointed.

So, for dealings to be carried on by God with His people, it could be done by no other means than the sacrifice.

Otherwise, the children of Israel would have been destroyed along with the Egyptians, etc.

A BETTER CONTRACT

Even though we presently have a much better contract, so to speak, due to Christ having gone to the Cross, still, God deals with us on the same basis as He did the children of Israel. It was faith then in the coming One, represented by the animal sacrifices, and it is faith, and faith alone, now in the One who has come (Gal. 5:5-6).

If we believe in the promises of God, in whatever capacity those promises might be, we must ever understand that they are based on the sacrifice of Christ, and the sacrifice of Christ alone! Our faith in the finished work of Christ presents itself as the key ingredient. Whatever the Word of God says that I can have, that is what I want, and I will obtain it by faith in the Cross. Everything He has personally guaranteed me, I will receive on the same basis, and that basis alone.

YOUR CHILDREN

"And it shall come to pass, when your children shall say unto you, What mean you by this service?" (Ex. 12:26).

In this passage, we are plainly told that it is our responsibility to properly relate and explain the great sacrifice of Christ to our children. This we must not fail to do.

Verse 26 plainly tells us that it is God's intention that

we relate to the children this simple yet grand and glorious story. They can well understand the doctrine of the expiatory sacrifice. In fact, it was meant to be a gospel, not only for the elder but, as well, for the youngest.

I was saved and baptized with the Holy Spirit when I was 8 years old.

While I did not remotely know and understand what I know and understand presently, still, at that tender age, I knew enough about the atonement, i.e., Jesus died for me, to respond favorably to Christ when He spoke to my heart through the person and agency of the Holy Spirit.

YOUNG PEOPLE

I grieve when I see the church trying to reach young people by using the things of the world. By that, I speak of the efforts to copy the rock shows, thinking this will draw youth to Christ.

How foolish can we be?

It is the Holy Spirit who convicts of sin, and the Holy Spirit alone. He does so on the gospel being given, and by the gospel, we speak of the preaching of the Cross (I Cor. 1:23; 2:2).

Over the SonLife Broadcasting Network, which covers a large part of the entirety of the world, we never use the music to try to reach a certain segment of people.

Rather, we do our best to be led by the Holy Spirit and to play the music that we feel the Lord would want.

We then let Him take care of the balance, for He alone can do such.

No, using the ways of the world definitely doesn't bring young people to Christ, or anyone else for that matter!

DELIVERANCE

"That you shall say, It is the sacrifice of the LORD's *Passover, who passed over the houses of the children of Israel in Egypt, when He smote the Egyptians, and delivered our houses. And the people bowed the head and worshipped. And the children of Israel went away, and did as the* LORD *had commanded Moses and Aaron, so did they"* (Ex. 12:27-28).

As is obvious, the Scripture plainly states here that it is *"the* LORD's *Passover,"* meaning that all, as it pertains to salvation, is of the Lord, and of the Lord alone!

The application of the blood spelled salvation for the children of Israel but destruction for the Egyptians. It is no less presently!

The Cross either saves or condemns, depending on acceptance or rejection.

If one rejects the Cross, then one faces the wrath of God, which no sane person wants to face.

God poured out His wrath upon His only Son, the Lord Jesus Christ, who was meant to be a substitute for the human race.

However, if men refuse to accept Him, they must expect

the wrath of God simply because *"the wrath of God is revealed from heaven against all ungodliness and unrighteousness of men, who hold the truth in unrighteousness"* (Rom. 1:18).

WORSHIP

When the people heard the instructions as given by Moses concerning the paschal lamb and how they would be delivered, the Scriptures say that they *"bowed the head and worshipped."*

This should ever be the response, even of modern believers, when the story of the Cross is related to us. It must never grow old, and must ever elicit worship from our hearts, and for all the obvious reasons.

One of the major problems in the modern church is worship based on something other than the Cross, which, in fact, God will not accept. Now, let the reader study these words very carefully.

It doesn't matter how much we run, jump, or leap, or what type of demonstration we may refer to as worship; if it's not based strictly on the Cross of Christ as Verse 27 proclaims, it's not acceptable to the Lord.

Regrettably, that means that most of the worship in the modern church is unacceptable.

What does it mean for our worship to be based on the fundamentals of the Cross?

It means simply that our faith is to ever be anchored in the Cross of Christ and that the Cross is to ever be our object.

This means that we understand that everything we receive from the Lord comes to us exclusively through the finished work of Christ and by no other means. This is the means by which the Holy Spirit works, and that type of understanding makes us acceptable to God, who then accepts our worship (Rom. 8:1-2).

OBEDIENCE

Upon hearing the instructions, as somber as they must have been, after they had worshipped the Lord, they then went away to do what the Lord had commanded that should be done.

This had to be one of the most solemn moments in history. It was taking these people to a place and position they had not heretofore been and, in fact, a place and position where no one had ever been.

In essence, the Cross was being presented to them and, in essence, it would effect their deliverance as well as the defeat of the Egyptians.

MIDNIGHT

"And it came to pass, that at midnight the LORD *smote all the firstborn in the land of Egypt, from the firstborn of Pharaoh who sat on his throne unto the firstborn of the captive that was in the dungeon; and all the firstborn of cattle"* (Ex. 12:29).

It is obvious that the day of this visitation had not been fixed. More than likely it took place on the 21ST day of the month or possibly on the 22ND day. The exact time was midnight.

All were affected, from the highest to the lowest. It even affected the firstborn of cattle, and probably all other animals, as well, inasmuch as the word cattle covered most all domestic animals.

Over and over again, Pharaoh had been warned, but to no avail. Now, not only would he have to pay for his obstinacy, but the entire nation of Egypt also.

That night, when the firstborns were to be destroyed, no Israelite could stir out of doors till toward morning when they would be called to march out of Egypt.

GOD MEANS WHAT HE SAYS
AND SAYS WHAT HE MEANS

Men must learn that God says what He means, but the trouble is, man is loath to take God at His Word.

Despite some nine astounding miracles, in fact, miracles of unprecedented proportions, it seems that Pharaoh simply did not believe that all the firstborn would die. It would seem to me that it would be impossible for him not to acquiesce if he actually believed that God was going to do this which Moses said.

Did he doubt the power of God? Did he doubt that God could do such a thing? It would seem that he had seen enough, as it regarded the miracles that had been performed, that he ought to know exactly what God could do.

The tenderest time for Pharaoh was after the first miracle was performed, but with each succeeding rejection, his heart became harder and harder, for that's what sin does to those who rebel against God.

Each negative answer carries with it a penalty of hardness that makes it more difficult the next time to yield.

I think it's possible that a person can become so hard because of rebellion that even though they may want to yield to the Lord, they simply do not have the capacity to do so anymore.

CHRISTIANS?

It is very possible for Christians to fall into the same trap. Little by little they cool off until they no longer sense or feel the presence of God. They can sit through service after service, even with God moving mightily, and it never seems to touch them. That's a very, very dangerous position for a Christian to find himself.

Such a position has little to do with what is actually happening. In other words, Judas lost his way right in the midst of the greatest move of God the world had ever known, and I speak of the ministry of the Master. If in that type of atmosphere, Judas could lose his way, which he did, we should well understand that it could very easily be done in present circumstances.

Why and how do Christians fall into such a trap? I think the reason is twofold:

1. Such a Christian ceases to look to the Cross, but rather to other things.

2. Such a Christian ceases to be diligent. Peter said: *"Wherefore, beloved, seeing that you look for such things, be diligent that you may be found of Him in peace, without spot, and blameless"* (II Pet. 3:14).

Living for the Lord is like a marriage. It has to be diligently attended, and one has to work at being what one ought to be. It's not that we earn something. That's not the idea at all!

However, the simple fact is, if we want to be the Christian we ought to be, we have to be diligent about that which is so very, very precious to us, or at least, it certainly should be.

> *I'm pressing on the upward way,*
> *New heights I'm gaining every day;*
> *Still praying as I'm onward bound,*
> *Lord, plant my feet on higher ground.*
>
> *My heart has no desire to stay,*
> *Where doubts arise and fears dismay;*
> *Though some may dwell where these abound,*
> *My prayer, my aim is higher ground."*
>
> *I want to live above the world,*
> *Though Satan's darts at me are hurled;*

For faith has caught the joyful sound,
The song of saints on higher ground.

I want to scale the utmost height,
And catch a gleam of glory bright;
But still I'll pray till heaven I've found,
Lord, lead me on to higher ground.

Lord lift me up and let me stand,
By faith on heaven's tableland,
A higher plane than I have found;
Lord, plant my feet on higher ground.

CHAPTER 2

JUDGMENT

JUDGMENT

"AND PHARAOH ROSE UP *in the night, he, and all his ser-vants, and all the Egyptians; and there was a great cry in Egypt; for there was not a house where there was not one dead" (Ex. 12:30).*

In the religion of the Egyptians (which was not true, nevertheless, they believed it anyway), the entirety of their being—past, present, and future—had just been decimated. By believing that the afterlife consisted of the prosperity of the firstborn, what had happened to them was tantamount to a Christian being consigned to eternal darkness—the loss of the soul. Understanding it in that fashion, we can see how the death of the firstborn affected the entirety of the nation of Egypt.

Exactly how these deaths came about, we aren't told; however, it should be obvious that the Lord could have brought about this tragedy in any number of ways. Again, let us emphasize the fact that none of this had to be. The Lord had the right to demand the release of His people, who, in fact, had been worked as slaves for over 100 years.

All Pharaoh had to do was obey, and all of this tragedy would have been avoided. However, we find that he wouldn't obey until he had no choice but to obey.

The great cry that filled Egypt that early morning hour was not only registered toward the tremendous loss that every house had experienced, but, as well, it was a demand that Pharaoh let the children of Israel go.

At the very beginning—weeks earlier—before even the first miracle had been performed, the very first message that the Lord commanded Moses to deliver to Egypt's ruler was, *"Thus says the LORD, Israel is My son, even My firstborn: And I say unto you, Let My son go, that he may serve Me: and if you refuse to let him go, behold, I will kill your son, even your firstborn"* (Ex. 4:22-23). So, as is overly obvious, Pharaoh was without excuse.

EXCEPT YOU REPENT

In reality, the message delivered and carried out then is the same presently. All through this Christian dispensation, the solemn word has been going forth, *"Except you repent, you shall all likewise perish"* (Lk. 13:3); *"He who believes not shall be damned"* (Mk. 16:16). However, even as with Pharaoh, for the most part, the divine warning has fallen on deaf ears. The vast majority does not believe that God means what He says.

While it is true that God is slow to anger, and long does He leave open the door of mercy, even His longsuffering has its limits. It was thus with Pharaoh and his people. Pharaoh received plain and faithful warning, and this was followed by many appeals and preliminary judgments. However, this haughty king and his no less defiant subjects only hardened their hearts. Now, the threatened judgments from heaven fell upon them, and neither wealth nor poverty provided any exemption—*"There was not a house where there was not one dead."*

Let those, even in this day of grace, take solemn warning. The message is no less now than then and, in fact, is even more so. In Old Testament times, it says that God winked at ignorance *"but now commands all men everywhere to repent,"* and that is because of the Cross (Acts 17:30).

JUDGMENT AND THE CROSS

God must judge sin, and, in fact, He has judged sin. He judged it by the smiting of His own Son (Isa. 53:4). In other words, the blow that we should have taken, He took in our place. The difference is, judgment upon us would not have effected salvation, while judgment upon Him paid the price for our sins, and faith expressed in Christ and what He did for us at the Cross guarantees redemption and exemption from the judgment of God.

Let the reader understand the following: Humanity accepts Christ and what He has done for us and, thereby, escapes judgment because, in fact, Jesus has already taken our judgment. Otherwise, judgment will come upon the

Christ-rejecter just as surely as it came upon Egypt of so long ago.

Let me say the following, and let me say it clearly: The only thing that stands between humanity and the judgment of almighty God is the Cross of Christ. Think about that statement, allow it to penetrate your heart, and understand the truthfulness of what is being said. If the Cross is rejected, then Christ is rejected. Let that be made abundantly clear. It is impossible to accept Christ, to know Christ, to have Christ, and to have and afford His salvation without accepting what He has done for us in the sacrifice of Himself on the Cross.

THE LIFE OF CHRIST

Mackintosh said: "True Christianity is but the manifestation of the life of Christ, implanted in us by the operation of the Holy Spirit, in pursuance of God's eternal counsels of sovereign grace; and all our doings previous to the implantation of this life are but 'dead works,' from which we need to have our consciences purged just as much as from 'wicked works'" (Heb. 9:14).

Let me say in following that statement that the only way that we can have the life of Christ implanted in us is by faith in Christ and the substitutionary offering of Himself on our behalf. Paul explained this graphically, which leaves no room for misunderstanding.

He said: *"Know you not, that so many of us as were baptized into Jesus Christ were baptized into His death?*

Therefore we are buried with Him by baptism into death: that like as Christ was raised up from the dead by the glory of the Father, even so we also should walk in newness of life. For if we have been planted together in the likeness of His death, we shall be also in the likeness of His resurrection" (Rom. 6:3-5).

BAPTIZED ...

First of all, let the reader understand that even though Paul used the word *baptized*, he was not at all speaking of water baptism. In fact, water baptism has absolutely nothing to do with this particular statement. He was speaking of the crucifixion, burial, and resurrection of Christ and our part in that great work, which comes to us by faith.

Let me explain: Jesus Christ was and is our substitute. In other words, He did for us what we could not do for ourselves.

When He died on the Cross, God, in a sense, looked at Him as being us, which we gain by faith.

Even though He definitely was punished on the Cross, punishment was not really the primary purpose of the crucifixion. The paying of the price, i.e., *"the paying of the ransom,"* is what the Cross was all about.

THE RANSOM

Jesus said of Himself: *"Even as the Son of Man came not to be ministered unto, but to minister, and to give His life a ransom for many"* (Mat. 20:28).

Paul said: *"For there is one God, and one media-
tor between God and men, the man Christ Jesus; who
gave Himself a ransom for all, to be testified in due time"*
(I Tim. 2:5-6).

Whenever the believing sinner expresses faith in Christ
and what Christ did at the Cross, in the mind of God, the
believing sinner is literally placed in Christ, in His death,
burial, and resurrection.

To explain this, the strongest word that could be used was
the word *baptized.* The word literally means that the person
is literally placed into that into which he is baptized, and that
into which he is baptized is placed into him. It's like a ship
that has sunk and goes to the bottom of the sea. The ship is in
the sea and the sea is in the ship, which is an apt description
of baptism.

The word *baptism* can be used in either a literal or a figurative sense. Here Paul is using it in the figurative sense.

To give you an example, the Scripture says, *"I indeed baptize you with water unto repentance* (John the Baptist uses
the word *baptize* here in the literal sense): *but He who comes
after me is mightier than I, whose shoes I am not worthy to
bear: He shall baptize you* (here he uses it in the figurative
sense) *with the Holy Spirit, and with fire"* (Mat. 3:11).

RESURRECTION PEOPLE?

Many presently are fond of claiming themselves to be

resurrection people. That is true after a fashion, but only if the correct meaning is understood.

Unfortunately, most of the time, when people use such a term concerning the resurrection, they are belittling the Cross.

Concerning the resurrection, the believer must know and understand the following: Paul plainly told us that while it is true that we are *"in the likeness of His resurrection,"* which definitely makes us resurrection people, we have this great privilege, this great glory and honor, which gives us power to live a resurrected life, simply because, *"we have been planted together in the likeness of His death"* (Rom. 6:5). In other words, the Cross is what made possible His resurrection and, as well, makes possible our resurrection life.

THE CROSS

It is the understanding of His death, which speaks of the crucifixion, what He accomplished there, and our part in that great work, which we gain by faith, that makes this resurrection life possible.

If we understand it in that fashion, then we have a proper understanding of the term "resurrection people," etc. He atoned for every sin on the Cross, which guaranteed His resurrection and our resurrection life.

The destroying angel passed through the land of Egypt to destroy all the firstborn, but Israel's firstborn escaped through the death of a divinely-provided substitute.

Saved by the blood of the Lamb, they were privileged to consecrate their ransomed lives to Him who had ransomed them. Thus, it was only as redeemed that they possessed life. The grace of God alone had made them to differ and had given them the place of living men in His presence.

In their case, assuredly, there was no room for boasting, for as to any personal merit or worthiness, we learn from the following chapter that they were put on a level with an unclean and worthless thing, as we shall see upon arriving at that study.

PHARAOH, MOSES, AND AARON

"And he called for Moses and Aaron by night, and said, Rise up, and get you forth from among my people, both you and the children of Israel; and go, serve the LORD, as you have said. Also take your flocks and your herds, as you have said, and be gone; and bless me also" (Ex. 12:31-32).

Before daylight, in fact, it was probably not long after midnight; whatever actually happened brought forth the realization that the firstborn in each house had suddenly died. So, before dawn, Pharaoh, having suffered the loss of his own son, evidently sent a delegation to Moses and Aaron.

The message was to the point: The children of Israel could leave, and they could also take their flocks and their herds. Trembling with fear, the monarch requested of Moses and Aaron that they bless him also. Exactly what he meant by that is anyone's guess.

As we have repeatedly said, the Passover, which was a type of the offering of Christ, spelled either redemption or judgment according to acceptance or rejection. For all who accept Christ and His Cross, there is redemption. For all who reject Christ and His Cross, there is judgment.

In a sense, Pharaoh is a type of Satan holding men in bondage and refusing to let them go. So, how is it that the Cross of Christ forces him to lift the bondage?

SATAN AND THE CROSS

While the Cross of Christ had everything to do with Satan, in a sense, it had nothing to do with him. No, that's not a contradiction.

Hear me out: Jesus didn't go to the Cross to appease Satan or to pay some type of ransom to Satan, as some teach. While He definitely paid a ransom, it was not to Satan, but rather to God.

In other words, the Cross was totally and completely of God and for God. The price that was paid was paid to God; and what was that price?

The price was death, but not just any death. It had to be the death of the Son of God, who was unsullied, untainted, and unspoiled, in other words, the perfect sacrifice.

Jesus was our substitute in totality (I Cor. 15:45-50). When He died, He did so, in a sense, in our place, but yet, it was a place that we never could have filled or fulfilled because we were sinful and, therefore, unacceptable.

In fact, His death was contrived. Jesus did not die as ordinary mortals die. Actually, no one really killed Him, as far as the act was concerned, even though murder was in their hearts. The truth is, He literally laid down His life and literally took it up again.

JESUS AND HIS LIFE

He said: *"No man takes it from Me, but I lay it down of Myself. I have power to lay it down, and I have power to take it again. This commandment have I received of My Father"* (Jn. 10:17-18). There is every evidence that the Holy Spirit hovered over Christ at the crucifixion and literally told Him when He could die.

The Scripture says: *"How much more shall the blood of Christ, who through the eternal Spirit* (Holy Spirit) *offered Himself without spot to God"* (Heb. 9:14).

When He died—even as the perfect sacrifice, which is what He was and was intended to be—His death atoned for all sin, i.e., paid for all sin—past, present, and future—at least for all who will believe. This addressed not only sins in the plural but also sin in principle (Jn. 1:29). In other words, Jesus did not merely address the symptoms, which would have been the case had He only dealt with sins, but He rather went to the heart of the matter—the cause of all sin—who is Satan.

Satan had a legal right to hold man in captivity as a result of sin. He gained this right at the fall.

When I say legal right, I mean that God gave him that right. However, when Jesus atoned for all sin, Satan lost that legal right.

So, due to what Christ did at the Cross, Satan has no choice but to let the believer go free. The bondage is broken.

FREEDOM

Isaiah described it in this manner: *"I the LORD have called You* (Christ) *in righteousness ... To open the blind eyes, to bring out the prisoners from the prison, and them who sit in darkness out of the prison house"* (Isa. 42:6-7).

Continuing to prophesy concerning Christ, the prophet said: *"The Spirit of the Lord GOD is upon Me; because the LORD has anointed Me ... To proclaim liberty to the captives, and the opening of the prison to them who are bound"* (Isa. 61:1).

Does the reader fully understand what is being said here? Do you fully know what the Lord has actually done?

This means—I speak of what Jesus did at the Cross—that, in fact, every single human being on the face of this earth has been set free from every single bondage of darkness, no matter how bad or horrible it might be. This means, also, that every homosexual and lesbian can be set free from that terrible bondage. As well, every drunkard can be set free, and every gambler can be set free. Every drug addict can be set free, and the bondage of nicotine is broken. Jealousy, envy, malice, hatred, racism, unforgiveness, etc., all and without exception have had their chains splintered. The door is thrown open to those who were bound, and the person who was once a captive can now go free.

All that has to be done is for Christ and His Cross to be accepted, and along with the freedom, eternal life will be granted, which, as Peter said, is *"joy unspeakable and full of glory"* (I Pet. 1:8).

With every sin atoned, Satan has lost his legal right to hold man captive. To obtain this benefit, faith alone is required, and, in fact, faith alone is accepted. However, it must be faith in Christ and the Cross.

QUITTING EGYPT

> *And the Egyptians were urgent upon the people, that they might send them out of the land in haste; for they said, We be all dead men. And the people took their dough before it was leavened, their kneadingtroughs being bound up in their clothes upon their shoulders. And the children of Israel did according to the word of Moses: and they borrowed of the Egyptians jewels of silver, and jewels of gold, and raiment: And the LORD gave the people favor in the sight of the Egyptians, so that they lent unto them such things as they required. And they spoiled the Egyptians* (Ex. 12:33-36).

Several things are said here:

- The Egyptians were begging the children of Israel to

leave. With the firstborn now dead, they, no doubt, feared that all the men of Egypt might die next. At this stage, they were not comfortable in taking any chances.

- The children of Israel were prepared and ready to go. They even had their bowls ready, in which they mixed up the dough in order to make bread.
- Last of all, the Egyptians thrust upon the Israelites gold and silver, along with beautiful clothing.

The word *borrowed* is an unfortunate translation. These items were not given with any thought that they would be returned, nor were they taken with any thought of returning them.

THE WAGES WOULD BE PAID

It was the Lord who put it in the hearts of the Egyptians to give freely to the Israelites, and for all the obvious reasons. By now, the Egyptians were so fearful of all Israelites that they did not want to do anything that would seem to be contrary, but rather that which was favorable.

Hitherto, the Israelites were not permitted to depart; now they were commanded to depart. Pharaoh was in such terror that he gave orders by night for this discharge, fearing that if he delayed any longer, he himself should fall. He sent them out not as men hated, as some pagan historians have represented this matter, but as men feared, as plainly discovered by the humble request of Pharaoh, *"Bless me also."*

As well, the Lord took care that the hard-earned wages of the Israelites should at last be paid, and that the people should be provided for their journey; consequently, they departed laden with the wealth of Egypt. Even though He may tarry long, to be sure, God will take care of His people.

Concerning modern believers, Paul said, *"And let us not be weary in well doing: for in due season we shall reap, if we faint not"* (Gal. 6:9).

If the Christian will believe God, place his or her faith exclusively in Christ and the Cross, then everything that Satan has taken in the past can be restored, and much more besides.

THE EXODUS

"And the children of Israel journeyed from Rameses to Succoth, about six hundred thousand on foot who were men, beside children. And a mixed multitude went up also with them; and flocks, and herds, even very much cattle" (Ex. 12:37-38).

This is, no doubt, the Rameses of Exodus 1:11. It was a new town built in the reign of Rameses II. It was actually now used as the capital.

Succoth seems to have been a town about 15 miles due south of Rameses.

There were upwards of 3 million Israelites that were scattered all over Egypt. Considering this, we are probably to suppose that the main body with Moses and Aaron started from Rameses. With the others obeying orders previously given, they would have started from all parts of Egypt, but more specifically, from Goshen, with them converging upon Succoth, which was the first rendezvous.

Each body of travelers would have been accompanied by its flocks and herds, as well as Egyptian sympathizers.

There was probably no marching along roads, with few then existing. Each company could spread itself out at its pleasure and go at its own pace. All knew the point of meeting and marched toward it, in converging lines, with there being little or no obstacle to hinder them.

The six hundred thousand men mentioned here would have been men of war between 20 and 50 years of age. You could add 600,000 women to that, along with all the children and those above 50 years of age.

Including the mixed multitude, there could well have been upward of 3 million people or more involved.

PREPARATION

"And they baked unleavened cakes of the dough which they brought forth out of Egypt, for it was not leavened; because they were thrust out of Egypt, and could not tarry, neither had they prepared for themselves any victual" (Ex. 12:39).

The idea of this verse is to proclaim the fact that they had been told to prepare to leave on very short notice. It takes awhile, several hours, for leaven to set up in dough. So, we learn from this that they didn't even have that much time. In fact, they were ordered to leave the very night of the Passover. The notice was probably given about daylight, and the great march began.

As we look back on this, we should realize that the account of these happenings, while definitely historical, is much more. In fact, every single thing that took place as recorded in the Word of God is a step closer to the redemption that we now enjoy. It didn't come easily, and neither was it simple.

So, when we read these accounts, we should always read them with the idea in mind that this is the story of redemption—a redemption that ultimately came to me and is the greatest thing that ever happened to me. Of course, I speak for every believer.

THE CONCLUSION OF THE DISPENSATION OF PROMISE

"Now the sojourning of the children of Israel, who dwelt in Egypt, was four hundred and thirty years. And it came to pass at the end of the four hundred and thirty years, even the selfsame day it came to pass, that all the hosts of the LORD went out from the land of Egypt. It is a night to be much observed unto the LORD for bringing them out from the land of Egypt: this is that night of the LORD to be observed of all the children of Israel in their generations" (Ex. 12:40-42).

The 430 years mentioned here began with Abraham

when he was 75 years old and called of God to leave Ur of the Chaldees to go unto a land that God would show him (Gen. 12:1-3). This was the dispensation of promise.

The actual fulfillment of the promise was Christ; however, for this promise to be realized, a people had to be prepared, and this is the account of that preparation. To these people, the law would be given that would institute the dispensation of law, which would last until Christ would come.

John said, *"For the law was given by Moses, but grace and truth came by Jesus Christ"* (Jn. 1:17).

THE ACTUAL TIME IN EGYPT

Verse 40 doesn't say that the children of Israel dwelt in Egypt for 430 years, but that the entirety of the time of their sojourning was that long. The whole of the sojourn was from the 75TH year of Abraham's life when he entered Canaan to this day of exodus. The entire sojourn took place in Mesopotamia, Syria, Canaan, Philistia, and Egypt. The actual time in Egypt was only 215 years, one-half of the 430 years of the whole.

The 430 years present the whole link of the dispensation of promise—from Abraham to Moses.

THE HOSTS OF THE LORD

Verse 41 refers to the Israelites as *"the hosts of the LORD,"* meaning that they belonged to Him.

Verse 42 proclaims the fact that this night—the night of the first Passover—presented itself as an astounding happening. It was to be celebrated in all generations. In fact, it was commanded that the Passover was to be kept yearly forever.

Concerning this, Matthew Henry said: "The great things God does for His people are not to be only a few days' wonder, but the remembrance of them is to be perpetuated throughout all ages, especially the work of our redemption by Christ."

He went on to say:

> This first Passover-night was a night of the Lord, much to be observed; but the last Passover-night, in which Christ was betrayed, and in which the first Passover, with the rest of the ceremonial institutions, was superseded and abolished, was a night of the Lord, much more to be observed; when a yoke, heavier than that of Egypt, was broken off our necks, and a land, better than that of Canaan, set before us. That first Passover was a temporal deliverance to be celebrated in their generations; this an eternal redemption to be celebrated in the praises of glorious saints, world without end.

TEMPORAL BLESSINGS

While the blessings of our redemption must ever be set before us and must ever be talked about, preached about, and celebrated in our songs and worship, we should, as well, not forget the temporal blessings. The Lord is constantly doing good things for us, of which we should constantly remind ourselves and constantly thank Him, who is the fount of all blessings.

In prayer, even on a daily basis, I will notice that the Holy Spirit will bring to my mind, even over and over again, the beautiful and wonderful things that the Lord has done for me, which elicits praise on my part, as well it should.

I sometimes think that future blessings are hindered by a failure to properly thank the Lord for past and present blessings. We must never forget what He has done, and to be sure, as stated, the Holy Spirit will constantly bring it to our attention, and He does that for a purpose.

THE PASSOVER

"And the LORD *said unto Moses and Aaron, This is the ordinance of the Passover: There shall no stranger eat thereof"* (Ex. 12:43).

The Passover, i.e., the crucifixion of our Lord, provides the foundation for this amazing deliverance.

The idea is, they were the Lord's by purchase—bought with a price—and that price was not *"corruptible things, as silver and gold ... But with the precious blood of Christ* (the Lamb)" (I Pet. 1:18).

This *"ordinance of the Passover"* was for Israel's guidance in the future.

We may wonder why the Lord gave these instructions

here instead of giving them at the time He gave the law, which would be some weeks later. There is a reason for that.

I think these instructions were given at this particular time, which may seem to have been inopportune and even premature, simply because the Lord wanted the children of Israel to know and realize that their deliverance had come about simply because of and through the Passover. He wanted them to realize its vast significance, which I think should be obvious, as it regarded all the instructions given.

The stranger was not to partake of the Passover unless he came under the auspices of the covenant, which entailed circumcision for the males, etc. In other words, it was available to all, but only under certain conditions.

The gospel of Jesus Christ presently is available to all but, again, only under certain conditions. There must be faith, and we speak of faith in Christ and His Cross. When there is proper faith, it will be obvious as to the work of the Lord that's carried out in such an individual's life.

CIRCUMCISION

"But every man's servant who is bought for money, when you have circumcised him, then shall he eat thereof. A foreigner and a hired servant shall not eat thereof" (Ex. 12:44-45).

Circumcision has its antitype in the Cross. The male alone was circumcised; the female was represented in the male. So, in the Cross, Christ represented His church, and, hence, the church is crucified with Christ. Nevertheless, she lives by the life of Christ, known and exhibited on earth through the power of the Holy Spirit.

The ordinance of circumcision formed the grand boundary line between the Israel of God and all the nations that were upon the face of the earth. The Cross of our Lord Jesus Christ forms the boundary between the church and the world.

While the rite of circumcision didn't save anyone, the idea was that faith had been enjoined in the acceptance of the covenant, with circumcision then applied.

It involved the cutting of the flesh, which, of necessity, occasioned the shedding of blood. It typified the separation of the individual from the world and its system, with the shedding of blood typifying the price that would be paid by Christ for the redemption of mankind.

In fact, circumcision was not something new, having been practiced by several heathen nations; however, these nations were not a part of the covenant of the Lord, which pertained only to Israel.

ISRAEL ALONE

First of all, the Feast of the Passover was for Israel alone; therefore, no stranger must participate. The reason is obvious. It was only the children of Abraham, the family of faith, who had participated in God's gracious deliverance, and they alone could commemorate it.

Secondly, no hired servant should eat the Passover. A hired servant is an outsider; he is actuated by self-interest. He works for pay. However, no such principle can find a place in that which speaks of redemption: *"to him who works not, but believes on Him who justifies the ungodly, his faith is counted for righteousness"* (Rom. 4:5).

Thirdly, no uncircumcised person could eat the Passover. This applied to Israel equally as much as to Gentiles. At that time, circumcision was the sign of the covenant, and now, only those who belong to the covenant of grace can feed upon Christ. Circumcision was God's sentence of death written upon nature. Circumcision has its antitype in the Cross (Col. 2:11-12).

A wall, one might say, was erected to shut out enemies, but the door was open to receive friends.

No hired servant (and it speaks again of strangers) could participate in the feast, but a bond servant who had been purchased and circumcised, and who was now one of the household, could. So, too, could the foreigner who sojourned with Israel, providing he would submit to the rite of circumcision.

In this, we have a blessed foreshadowing of grace reaching out to the Gentiles, who though by nature were *"aliens from the commonwealth of Israel, and strangers from the covenants of promise,"* are now by grace, *"no more strangers and foreigners, but fellow citizens with the saints, and of the household of God"* (Eph. 2:12, 19)—a statement which manifestly looks back to Exodus, Chapter 12.

NO BROKEN BONES

"In one house shall it be eaten; you shall not carry forth ought of the flesh abroad out of the house; neither shall you break a bone thereof. All the congregation of Israel shall keep it" (Ex. 12:46-47).

The flesh of the Passover (the lamb) was not to be taken out of the house, but rather eaten in the house, typifying the fact that none are saved outside of the family of God.

Paul said: *"For every house is built by some man; but He who built all things is God. And Moses verily was faithful in all his house, as a servant, for a testimony of those things which were to be spoken after; but Christ as a Son over His own house; whose house are we, if we hold fast the confidence and the rejoicing of the hope firm unto the end"* (Heb. 3:4-6).

The house, of course, is Christ. Let it be known that there is no salvation out of this house.

This means that all who subscribe to Islam, Buddhism, Shintoism, Confucianism, Hinduism, Catholicism, Mormonism, or any form of Christianity that is corrupt cannot be saved.

As stated, outside of this house, there is no salvation, as there can be no salvation. It is Christ and Him crucified, or else, it is spiritual ruin and wreckage.

It is certainly true that at times, people who belong to one of these religions give their hearts to Christ and are, thereby, saved.

However, the fact is, if they have truly been saved, they are going to have to leave that religion, whatever it might be. For instance, there are many Catholics over a span of time who have given their hearts and lives to Christ and have truly been born again.

However, to maintain their walk with the Lord, they have to leave out of Catholicism.

No one can continue to engage himself in false doctrine—and virtually all of Catholicism is false—and maintain salvation. It cannot be.

The Scripture still says:

> *Be not unequally yoked together with unbelievers: for what fellowship has righteousness with unrighteousness? and what communion has light with darkness? And what concord has Christ with Belial? or what part has he who believes with an infidel? And what agreement has the temple of God with idols? for you are the temple of the living God; as God has said, I will dwell in them, and walk in them; and I will be their God, and they shall be My people. Wherefore come out from among them, and be you separate, saith the Lord, and touch not the unclean thing; and I will receive you* (II Cor. 6:14-17).

I don't think it could be clearer than what Paul has said. Let's say it again: There can be no salvation outside of this house.

ANOTHER JESUS

The greatest problem in Christianity, which has existed from the days of the early church, is the problem of the church worshipping and serving *"another Jesus."*

Concerning this, Paul also said, *"For if he who comes preaching another Jesus, whom we have not preached, or if you receive another spirit, which you have not received, or another gospel, which you have not accepted, you might well bear with him"* (II Cor. 11:4).

To the Galatians, he basically said the same thing:

"I marvel that you are so soon removed from Him who called you into the grace of Christ unto another gospel: Which is not another; but there be some who trouble you, and would pervert the Gospel of Christ" (Gal. 1:6-7).

What was Paul talking about as it regards these statements?

Very adamantly, he also said, *"For Christ sent me not to baptize, but to preach the Gospel: not with wisdom of words, lest the Cross of Christ should be made of none effect"* (I Cor. 1:17).

In fact, to Paul was given the responsibility by Christ of being the founder of the church, so to speak. He referred to himself as the *"masterbuilder"* (I Cor. 3:10).

THE FOUNDATION OF THE CROSS

Concerning that responsibility, he also said: *"For other foundation can no man lay than that is laid, which is Jesus*

Christ" (I Cor. 3:11). In essence, this also says, *"Jesus Christ and Him crucified."*

Paul established the churches on the foundation of the Cross, but regrettably, so-called Christian Jews came out of Jerusalem and Judaea and ministered in these churches established by Paul, or those in association with Paul.

Of course, they did this after Paul had gone on to other fields of labor.

These interlopers claimed to believe in Christ, claimed to accept Christ, and claimed Christ as the Messiah; however, they also claimed that in order for one to be saved, one, as well, had to keep the law of Moses.

That's why Paul strongly stated, *"For in Jesus Christ neither circumcision avails anything, nor uncircumcision; but faith which works by love"* (Gal. 5:6).

In fact, he wrote the entirety of the epistle to the Galatians to counteract this false teaching.

So, in essence, what these people were preaching was another Jesus, which refers to Jesus being held up in any manner other than *"Jesus Christ and Him crucified."*

In fact, that was not only the great sin of the early church, it is also the great sin presently. In most churches, and I think I exaggerate not, the Jesus who is preached is not the Jesus of the Cross, but rather another Jesus.

If another Jesus is preached, the people will not receive the moving and operation of the Holy Spirit, but rather "another spirit."

All of this will constitute "another gospel."

HOW MANY CHURCHES ARE PRESENTLY PREACHING THE CROSS?

The Catholic Church actually preaches the church, in a sense, claiming that the church saves, which means it is not preaching Christ. So, whatever Jesus they do preach is "another Jesus."

The Protestant world is divided basically into three classes:

1. The modernists: These people do not believe the Bible to be the Word of God, nor do they believe that Jesus Christ is the Son of God. In fact, they don't believe much of anything. Regrettably and sadly, they probably make up about 50 to 70 percent of that which refers to itself as Christianity.

2. Those who preach the Cross for salvation: There are many Protestant churches that fall into this category, and thank God that they do preach this. They somewhat understand the Cross as it refers to salvation but understand it not at all as it refers to sanctification, in other words, how we live for God on a daily basis. Consequently, the people who attend these churches, for the most part, live defeated Christian lives.

3. Those who preach the Cross for both salvation and sanctification: Actually, this is the message that Paul preached, which means that it is the correct message. Anyone who has the privilege of attending a church of this nature is privileged indeed! There

aren't many preachers preaching this message, the Message of the Cross, but thank God for those who are, and thankfully, the number is increasing steadily.

LEGALISM, ANTINOMIANISM, AND GALATIANISM

It probably can be said without any fear of contradiction that the entirety of the world, in one way or the other, falls into one of these three categories. To be frank, most Christians have probably never even heard of antinomianism or Galatianism. Whether the words are familiar or not isn't that important, but what they mean is very, very important.

Let's break them down, and perhaps their meanings might be of help to you, the reader, as it refers to understanding the Word of God and how Satan seeks to pervert the gospel.

LEGALISM

In fact, most of the world falls under the category of legalism in one way or the other. I refer not only to professed Christianity but, as well, to the other major religions, or to one's own private religion that he has devised out of his own mind. This applies to many in the world.

To make it simple and easy to understand, I have often referred to legalism as the brownie point system. In other words, individuals think they are saved or have attained some type of religious position according to good things they do or bad things they don't do. In one way or another, almost the entirety of the world functions on this particular basis.

Even those who do not know anything at all about the Bible and are not even certain if there is a God, much less a heaven or a hell, will often say, "I think I'm alright, whatever there is out there after death," or words to that effect. As stated, they are basing their thoughts on good things they claim to do or bad things they claim to not have done.

These people do not trust Christ at all and, in fact, don't even believe in Christ.

Going 180 degrees from Christianity, we look for a moment at the world of Islam. This particular religion is strictly a form of legalism. When Muslims attempt to kill others who oppose their religion, they are taught that this is a good deed that will guarantee themselves a place in heaven, etc. Most other religions, although not this militant, function somewhat in the same manner, at least as far as works are concerned.

WORKS

Christians have to be very careful, as well, that their faith is not placed in works, but rather in Christ and what He has done for us at the Cross.

In fact, this is probably the greatest battle in Christianity simply because the doing of good things constitutes that which is good, at least good in our sight. We tend to think of it as earning us something with God.

It doesn't!

The sadness is, most Christians will agree with what I've just said and then turn right around and place their faith in works. All of this is legalism.

For instance, the restoration process of the modern church is mostly unscriptural. It is unscriptural because it is anchored in works and not at all in faith. Pure and simple, it is legalism. In other words, you are righteous if you do these particular things (I speak of works devised by men) and if you don't do those particular things, you are unrighteous.

ANTINOMIANISM

In the Greek, *anti* means, "to be against." The word *nomi* in the Greek means "law." So, the word *antinomianism* means "against law."

At first glance, that might seem to be correct; however, what such people who practice antinomianism are actually doing is taking liberty into license.

Paul faced this same problem in the early church exactly as he did the problems of legalism and Galatianism. He had stated, *"But where sin abounded, grace did much more abound"* (Rom. 5:20).

Some of the Christians of that particular time took his statement to excess. In other words, they surmised that due to the fact that grace was so abundant and so powerful, it didn't really matter about sin.

In other words, they could do whatever it was they wanted to do without any fear of repercussions.

The apostle answered that by saying: *"What shall we say then? Shall we continue in sin, that grace may abound? God forbid. How shall we, who are dead to sin, live any longer therein?"* (Rom. 6:1-2).

In fact, the church is full of these types of people presently. They have the erroneous conclusion that sin doesn't matter and that grace automatically covers their sin the moment that it is committed, and so it's no big deal.

In other words, they are lawless.

LIBERTY

Paul further answered that by saying: *"All things are lawful unto me, but all things are not expedient: all things are lawful for me, but I will not be brought under the power of any"* (I Cor. 6:12).

The true Christian must always understand that liberty, as it is given to him by Christ, refers to liberty to live a holy life and not liberty to sin. In fact, the Cross of Christ is God's answer to sin, which means that the Cross not only atoned for all sin, but, as well, faith in that finished work of Christ gives us victory over all sin, which refers to the sanctification of the saint.

As a believer, I am definitely subject to the moral law, which should be obvious, but I'm not subject to that moral law as it refers to commandments. Jesus has answered all of that, and if my faith is properly in Him and what He has done for me at the Cross, the Holy Spirit will then work powerfully within my heart and life and I can, thereby, keep the moral law in every respect without difficulty.

CRUCIFIED WITH CHRIST

There are many things as a Christian that I won't do, even as Paul said, because it's not expedient. In other words, it doesn't bring glory to God. I never think about these things but only my faith in Christ and His finished work. It then becomes easy to live this Christian life. However, if we try to do so by means of keeping commandments, etc., we will quickly find ourselves in a perilous situation.

Concerning this, Paul also said: *"I am crucified with Christ* (trusting in what Christ did at the crucifixion): *nevertheless I live* (am able to live this Christian life); *yet not I* (meaning that he cannot live this life within his own ability and strength), *but Christ lives in me* (and does so by virtue of the Cross and my faith in that finished work): *and the life which I now live in the flesh* (my everyday walk before God) *I live by the faith of the Son of God* (faith in Christ and what He has done for me at the Cross), *who loved me, and gave Himself for me."*

He then said: *"I do not frustrate the grace of God* (by trying to live a 'works' religion): *for if righteousness come by the law* (the believer trying to earn righteousness by keeping laws), *then Christ is dead in vain* (if one can attain to righteousness by keeping laws, then Christ died on the Cross needlessly)" (Gal. 2:20-21).

As a Christian, I'm definitely not against the laws of God, but I address those laws through Christ and not at all by my own strength, etc.

GALATIANISM

Galatianism refers to the teaching that Paul gave us in his epistle to the Galatians.

These people had been saved by faith but now were trying to sanctify themselves by works. They were doing this because of false teachers who had come in, claiming that they had to also keep the law, etc.

I think that one could say without fear of contradiction that Galatianism is the greatest problem for the true child of God. Why is it such a great problem?

Almost every true Christian understands the Cross, at least up to a point, as it regards salvation; however, most know absolutely nothing about the Cross as it regards sanctification. There, they draw a blank.

The major problem is, most Christians are loath to admit that they lack understanding as it regards the Cross. They look at the Cross as something that's elementary, thereby, having learned all about that when they first got saved.

Just yesterday, a dear brother was in my office and mentioned to me that it was very hard for him to admit that when he first began to hear us teach about the Cross, he was bereft of this great knowledge. He, as most Christians, had been living for God for many, many years.

In fact, he definitely was and is a very dedicated Christian. So, the idea that he didn't understand all about the Cross, at least at first, was very difficult for him to admit. Regrettably, it is the same with most Christians.

PAUL'S EPISTLE TO THE ROMANS

The truth is, very few Christians, including preachers, understand the Cross of Christ as it regards sanctification. In other words, they simply don't know what Romans, Chapters 6, 7, and 8 actually mean.

In fact, most preachers interpret Romans, Chapter 6, as Paul referring to water baptism (Rom. 6:3-5). Consequently, inasmuch as they have already been baptized in water, they somewhat write off the entire chapter as not applying to them.

Paul was not speaking of water baptism in these passages, but rather the crucifixion of Christ. We are baptized into His death, His burial, and His resurrection.

He used the word *baptized* in a figurative sense instead of the literal sense.

He did so because this word *baptized* describes the experience with Christ and what He did for us at the Cross, and our part in Him, as no other word does.

Incidentally, the word *baptized* in Matthew 3:11 is used both literally and figuratively.

Then we have Romans, Chapter 7. The group that subscribes to antinomianism uses Romans, Chapter 7, as their foundational text, claiming that one cannot help but sin, etc.

Romans 7:15 is their often used text: *"For that which I do I allow not* (understand not): *for what I would, that do I not; but what I hate, that do I."*

Another group relegates Chapter 7 of Romans to Paul's experience before conversion, so they just pass it off in that fashion, thereby, little understanding what the apostle was saying.

WHAT PAUL ACTUALLY TAUGHT

No, in Romans, Chapter 7, Paul was not teaching that Christians have to sin a little bit every day, and neither was he giving his experience before conversion.

In fact, Paul was dealing with his experience after conversion, after being baptized with the Holy Spirit, and after beginning to preach the gospel.

Not understanding the Cross, and we speak of the time frame after his conversion, he tried to live for God the way most Christians do, which refers to keeping rules and regulations.

He found that he couldn't carry out the task as he should, which left him in a very perilous situation: *"O wretched man that I am! Who shall deliver me from the body of this death?"* (Rom. 7:24).

Out of that desperation, the Lord gave to Paul the revelation of the Cross, which, in effect, is the meaning of the new covenant, which he then gave to us in his 14 epistles.

However, getting back to our original thought, not

understanding the Cross as it refers to sanctification—because most don't understand what Paul taught about this all-important subject—most Christians seek to sanctify themselves, and to do so by a regimen of works. God can never sanction such simply because when we do this, we are, in fact, practicing spiritual adultery (Rom. 7:1-4). Regrettably, this is the position of most modern Christians.

GRACE

Grace is simply the goodness of God extended to undeserving people. More than all, it is the Holy Spirit carrying out all the benefits of the Cross within our hearts and lives, at least if we allow Him to do such.

The grace of God is made possible by the Cross.

In fact, God has always had grace and has always functioned in grace.

In truth, the Lord doesn't have any more grace presently, even though this is the dispensation of grace, than He did in Old Testament times. The problem in Old Testament times was, due to the fact that the blood of bulls and goats couldn't take away sins, God was limited as to the grace He could extend to individuals.

Since the Cross, which paid the terrible sin debt and is the key to the great plan of salvation, the grace of God can now be extended to believers in an uninterrupted flow.

For that flow to continue uninterrupted, it only requires that we have faith in Christ and what Christ has done for us at the Cross, ever making that the object of our faith. Then the Holy Spirit works mightily within us, continuing to extend to us the grace of God.

In fact, the Cross and grace are forever interlocked. The believer cannot have one without the other.

One of the reasons that there is very little grace that is evident is because of a lack of understanding of the Cross.

A CONSTANT FLOW OF THE GRACE OF GOD

Not understanding the Cross, most have a confused idea of grace, even referring to such as "greasy grace," "easy grace," etc. Were it not for ignorance, such would border on blasphemy!

It is impossible for the believer to live a victorious life without a constant flow of the grace of God.

This means that the Holy Spirit has to constantly help us. In fact, without Him and His work, we can do nothing. This is what Jesus meant when He said: *"I am the vine, you are the branches: he who abides in Me, and I in him, the same brings forth much fruit: for without Me you can do nothing"* (Jn. 15:5).

When He used the phrase, *"For without Me you can do nothing,"* He was referring to what He carries out within our lives through the person, work, agency, and power of the Holy Spirit.

He also said: *"If any man thirst, let him come unto Me, and drink. He who believes on Me, as the Scripture has said, out of his belly* (innermost being) *shall flow rivers of living water.* (But this spoke He of the Spirit)" (Jn. 7:37-39).

When Jesus spoke in this manner, referring to Himself as the fountain and source of all life, which He definitely is, He was referring to what He did at the Cross, which made it all possible.

The Holy Spirit works very closely with Him, constantly glorifying Christ, and always working within the parameters of the finished work of Christ.

That's what Paul was meaning when he said: *"For the law of the Spirit of life in Christ Jesus has made me free from the law of sin and death"* (Rom. 8:2).

This *"law of the Spirit of life,"* of course, refers to the Holy Spirit, but the phrase, *"in Christ Jesus,"* refers to Christ and what Christ did at the Cross, as proven by the little word *in.*

FRUSTRATING THE GRACE OF GOD

Paul also said: *"I do not frustrate the grace of God: for if righteousness come by the law, then Christ is dead in vain"* (Gal. 2:21).

We are plainly told here that it is possible to frustrate the grace of God. When this is done, the grace of God is greatly hindered in its coming to us, or it could even be stopped. We are then left on our own.

This means that we do not have the help of the Holy Spirit, which guarantees failure.

So, how can a Christian frustrate the grace of God?

We frustrate the grace of God when we attempt to live for God by means of keeping laws, etc.

In other words, if we're trying to live for the Lord by any method other than simple faith in Christ and what Christ has done for us at the Cross, all we will succeed in doing is to frustrate the grace of God, which means to greatly hinder its flow.

As we've already stated, to have an uninterrupted flow of grace, all we have to do is have faith in Christ and His great sacrifice of Himself, and continue to have faith in that respect, ever making the Cross of Christ the object of our faith. Then the grace of God will flow to us like a river, and we will find that living for the Lord then becomes a joy instead of a chore.

We will also find ourselves overcoming every sin, transgression, and iniquity with which we have had great problems in the past.

In fact, this is the only way that the believer can live a victorious, overcoming, Christian life.

NO BROKEN BONE

Concerning the Passover, the Scripture plainly said that the children of Israel were not to break a single bone in the partaking of this feast. What did that represent?

It referred to Christ. The Spirit of prophecy, concerning Christ, had David to write: *"He keeps all His bones: not one of them is broken"* (Ps. 34:20).

When Jesus was crucified, *"The Jews therefore, because it was the preparation, that the bodies should not remain upon the Cross on the Sabbath day (for that Sabbath day was an high day,) besought Pilate that their legs might be broken, and that they might be taken away"* (Jn. 19:31).

Here was Satan in his malignant enmity attempting to falsify and nullify the written Word. Vain effort was it.

"Then came the soldiers, and broke the legs of the first, and of the other which was crucified with Him" (Jn.19:32).

THE WHOLENESS OF CHRIST

Concerning this, Pink said:

> Thus far might the agents of the Roman Empire go, but no farther – 'But when they came to Jesus, and saw that He was dead already, they broke not His legs' (Jn. 19:33). Here we are given to see the Father 'keeping' all the bones of His blessed Son. Pierce His side with a spear a soldier might, and this, only that prophecy might be fulfilled, for it was written, 'They shall look on Him whom they pierced' (Zech. 12:10). But break His legs they could not, for 'a bone of Him shall not be broken,' and it was not!

The bones not being broken carried the idea of the wholeness of Christ. While they might do all types of other things to Him, the initial frame of His sinless, perfect body was not broken.

This signified that He would carry out all that He had come to do, which He, in fact, did. Consequently, when we accept Christ, we do not accept a broken Christ, but rather the whole Christ, who gave Himself for us (Gal. 1:4).

As His personal body was one (unbroken), likewise, His church is one as well.

It is to be unbroken, referring to the fact that the true church, irrespective as to what name it has, is one with Christ by one simple method, and that is faith in Christ and His Cross.

CIRCUMCISION

"And when a stranger shall sojourn with you, and will keep the Passover to the LORD, let all his males be circumcised, and then let him come near and keep it; and he shall be as one who is born in the land: for no uncircumcised person shall eat thereof" (Ex. 12:48).

Several things are said in this verse:

- The word stranger refers to Gentiles, meaning that Gentiles could definitely come into the covenant, that is, if they came God's way.
- If they entered the covenant, all the males in that particular family would have to engage in the rite of circumcision. As previously stated, this concerned itself with separation of the flesh and the shedding of blood.

The separation, which circumcision entailed, pertains in

the spiritual sense to the believer separating himself from the efforts of the flesh and depending totally on the Spirit.

Once again, we go back to the Cross.

The shedding of blood, which always accompanied circumcision, pertained to the price that would be paid by the coming Redeemer, the Lord Jesus Christ, in His death on the Cross, which, of course, necessitated the shedding of His blood.

- Having done this, the stranger was, in fact, no more a stranger but was to be treated as "one who is born in the land." In other words, in the eyes of God, he had now become a Jew.

- If one refused to do this which was commanded by the Lord, he was not to be allowed to partake of the Passover, which meant that he wasn't saved.

ONE LAW

"One law shall be to him who is homeborn, and unto the stranger who sojourns among you" (Ex. 12:49).

The Lord doesn't have two ways of salvation, only one. That is Christ, even as it has always been Christ.

In fact, Paul asked the question and made the statement: *"What then? are we better than they? (Are Jews better than Gentiles?) No, in no wise: for we have before proved both Jews and Gentiles, that they are all under sin"* (Rom. 3:9).

Under the old law (the law of Moses), the Holy Spirit said

that Gentiles had to come in the same way as the Jews.

Under grace, the Holy Spirit says that Jews have to come the same way as Gentiles.

There's only one way, and that is Christ and Him crucified, irrespective of the person or his nationality.

DELIVERANCE

"Thus did all the children of Israel; as the LORD *commanded Moses and Aaron, so did they. And it came to pass the selfsame day, that the* LORD *did bring the children of Israel out of the land of Egypt by their armies"* (Ex. 12:50-51).

The words in Verse 51, *"the selfsame day,"* indicate that Abraham began his sojourn on the 15th day of Nisan, or our April, exactly 430 years before the exodus.

The word *armies* refers to the fact that the people were organized as they came out of Egypt, which means they did not come out as a rabble.

As well, God looked at them as armies simply because He was their captain, and through Him, they possessed great power.

The leaders of Egypt, at least at the beginning, had probably laughed at the demands of Moses, maybe even asking the question of where the army of Israel was that would free them from the land of Egypt.

Well, the Lord would show Egypt just exactly who this army was and the source of their power.

Days are filled with sorrow and care,
Hearts are lonely and drear;
Burdens are lifted at Calvary,
Jesus is very near.

Cast your care on Jesus today,
Leave your worry and fear;
Burdens are lifted at Calvary,
Jesus is very near.

Troubled soul, the Saviour can see,
Every heartache and tear;
Burdens are lifted at Calvary,
Jesus is very near.

WHEN I
SEE
THE
BLOOD

CHAPTER 3

A LAND FLOWING WITH
MILK AND HONEY

A LAND FLOWING WITH MILK AND HONEY

"**AND THE LORD SPOKE** *unto Moses, saying, Sanctify unto Me all the firstborn, whatsoever opens the womb among the children of Israel, both of man and of beast: It is Mine"* (Ex. 13:1-2).

The firstborns were to be sanctified unto the Lord, which means set apart unto the Lord, because they were to be a representation or a type of Christ. They were to be a picture of the salvation plan. Jesus is referred to as *"the firstborn among many brethren"* (Rom. 8:29).

Immediately after Israel was redeemed out of Egypt, instructions were given respecting the annual observance of the Passover. That is to say, Israel was to perpetually confess to the world that her salvation out of Egypt and her settlement in Canaan were wholly due to the preciousness of the blood of the paschal lamb.

Jesus being the firstborn doesn't mean that Jesus was "born again" after the crucifixion as some teach, but rather that He was the originator or the father, one might say, of the salvation experience. This means that through the Cross, He made salvation possible, even for the worst sinner.

WHETHER ISRAEL OR THE CHURCH, ALL ARE TO PORTRAY CHRIST

The whole of Israel was to be a type of Christ, with the firstborn being an even greater type. This extended, as is obvious here, even to the firstborn of animals. If it belonged to Israel, the type was to carry all the way through, even to that which they possessed, at least as far as the animals were concerned.

I want the reader to notice that even before the children of Israel were delivered from Egyptian bondage, instructions were being given to them that were very detailed regarding character and scope. These people had been raised up for a particular purpose, and that was, in effect, to serve as the womb of the Messiah. They were to also give the world the Word of God, which they did do.

However, as Israel was in the world, the church is to be as well. The difference is, the Word of God has already been given, and the church is to exemplify that Word. Also, Christ has already come, so the church is to portray Christ. Whether Israel or the church, all are to portray Christ, and above all, what He did at the Cross on behalf of lost humanity.

Mackintosh said, "As we've already stated, true Christianity is but the manifestation of the life of Christ, implanted in us by the operation of the Holy Spirit."

DELIVERED FROM THE HOUSE OF BONDAGE

"And Moses said unto the people, Remember this day, in which you came out from Egypt, out of the house of bondage; for by strength of hand the LORD brought you out from this place: there shall no leavened bread be eaten. This day came you out in the month Abib" (Ex. 13:3-4).

Israel was to understand, and to understand fully, that they had been delivered out of this house of bondage, not by their own ingenuity, strength, ability, or talent, but by the strength of the hand of the Lord.

There was no way they could have extricated themselves from this bondage, and even with God, it took His miracle-working power.

In essence, the Lord was telling the Israelites that they were now His people, for He had bought them, and they were, therefore, to be holy. They had been slaves to Pharaoh, but now, they were to be slaves to Jehovah.

However, as the Master would say: *"Take My yoke upon you, and learn of Me; for I am meek and lowly in heart: and you shall find rest unto your souls. For My yoke is easy, and My burden is light"* (Mat. 11:29-30).

Due to that yoke being easy and that burden being light, many, if not most, little function as they should. We take the blessings of the Lord for granted, actually demanding much, and give Him precious little in return. Perhaps that is the case with all of us.

At the least, I think one can say without any fear of

contradiction that the best among us, whomever that might be, little serves as we should.

A redeemed people become the property of the redeemer, which should be obvious. Consequently, the first exhortation in Romans, which follows the doctrinal exposition in Chapters 1 through 11, is, *"I beseech you therefore, brethren, by the mercies of God, that you present your bodies a living sacrifice, holy, acceptable unto God, which is your reasonable service"* (Rom. 12:1).

Personal devotion is the first thing that God has a right to expect from His blood-bought people.

THIS DAY

Verse 4 specifies that on a certain day, even in a certain month, the children of Israel were brought out of Egyptian bondage.

This tells us in no uncertain terms that salvation is not merely a philosophical quest, but rather a genuine know-so salvation. In other words, the believing sinner knows the exact moment that Christ comes into his heart.

At that moment, in the portals of glory, the Lord writes down the name of that individual in the Lamb's Book of Life. Forever, that date, time, and place are written down in glory so that it can be forever said, *"This day came you out."*

Oh, how I sense the presence of God even as I dictate these words. How so much the Lord has done for us; how so great is His salvation; and how so glorious is the moment we passed from death to life, from darkness to light, and from sin to salvation!

UNLEAVENED BREAD

As the following verses explain, the instruction given here pertaining to unleavened bread concerned itself with that feast which was to take place every year at the time of the Passover. During this time, no leavened bread was to be eaten because this bread represented Christ, who is perfect, sinless, holy, undefiled, etc.

Christ was the deliverer of the children of Israel, as He is the Saviour of all who trust in His name. As well, He delivered them by and through the type of the shed blood of the lamb.

In effect, one might say that they were delivered on credit, awaiting the day when He would come to this world and die on a Cross, thereby, taking away all sin (Jn. 1:29).

In fact, all seven of the great feasts of Israel, which were conducted at three different times of the year, required a male of every house to attend. All of these feasts, and without exception, proclaimed Christ and His expiatory, substitutionary work.

A LAND FLOWING WITH MILK AND HONEY

"And it shall be when the LORD shall bring you into the land of the Canaanites, and the Hittites, and the Amorites,

and the Hivites, and the Jebusites, which He swore unto your fathers to give you, a land flowing with milk and honey, that you shall keep this service in this month" (Ex. 13:5).

Several things are said in this passage:

- Without fail, the Lord would bring them into the Land of Promise. Regrettably, because of unbelief, Israel would take some 40 years to arrive there when they should have taken only about two years or less. In fact, the only thing that hinders the Lord is unbelief.

- While it is true that the land was filled with enemies, the Lord specifically stated that He would give this land unto them, which meant that He would defeat all of their enemies. The difference now is, He has already defeated all of these enemies; therefore, we make a sad mistake when we try to fight this battle all over again, as many of us have done. The victory is not ours to obtain for the simple reason that it is victory already possessed. We have it, and we maintain it by simply trusting in Christ and what Christ has done for us at the Cross.

- The Word of God has been given *"which He swore unto your fathers to give you,"* and it was, therefore, guaranteed of fulfillment.

THE PERFECTION OF CHRIST

- Furthermore, it was a land *"flowing with milk and*

honey." Everything that God gives is glorious, wonderful, and good. In fact, He has absolutely nothing that is bad in any respect. While He definitely does demand that we give up some things, what He gives us to take their place is so much more than what we lose that there is no comparison. Regrettably, at times, we sully His great and glorious gifts, but the fault is ours and not His.

- During the month of Abib (Nisan) each and every year, this great deliverance was to be celebrated by three particular feasts. It was to be the Feast of Passover, the Feast of Unleavened Bread, and the Feast of Firstfruits.

The first feast pictured Christ as the deliverer of His people, and the price He would pay on the Cross for that deliverance.

The second feast portrayed the perfection of Christ, which made the sacrifice of Himself acceptable.

The third feast pictured His resurrection.

So, we have death, perfection, and resurrection.

A FEAST TO THE LORD

"Seven days you shall eat unleavened bread, and in the seventh day shall be a feast to the LORD. Unleavened bread shall be eaten seven days; and there shall no leavened bread be seen with you, neither shall there be leaven seen with you

in all your quarters" (Ex. 13:6-7).

In fact, this Feast of Unleavened Bread lasted throughout the entirety of the seven days, but the first day and the last were to be kept especially holy (Lev. 23:6-8).

These injunctions have, in fact, already been given in Exodus, Chapter 12 (Vss. 15, 19). It was repeated, no doubt, in order to deepen the impression that the lesson the Holy Spirit desired to be taught would be amply learned.

The number seven here is not without significance. As used in the Word of God, it portrays in its final analysis the glory, totality, and perfection of the Lord Jesus Christ. In fact, all of these feasts, as given by God to Israel, were meant to portray the ministry of Christ in some fashion, which we will more fully explain when we come to the installations of the feasts in the giving of the law (Ex., Chpt. 23; Lev., Chpt. 23).

THE SEVENTH DAY

The seventh day of the seven days, which was deemed as a special day, refers to the finished work of Christ in that His mission would be a completed mission.

The unleavened bread, as sated, signified the perfection of Christ as it regarded His perfect body, perfect mind, and perfect actions.

In other words, there was no sin in Him.

The Scripture says of Him that He was and is *"holy, harmless, undefiled, separate from sinners, and made higher than the heavens"* (Heb. 7:26).

Leaven is used in the Old Testament and, as well, by Paul as a type of sin (Gal. 5:9). So, during these seven days, unleavened bread only was to be eaten, which typified that the coming Messiah would have no sin.

CHRIST IN US

Even though all of this typifies Christ, even as it is meant to do, at the same time, it typifies the sanctification of the believer for all of us, at least all who are born again who are in Christ.

To eat unleavened bread signifies separation from all evil in order that we may feed upon Christ. That this feast lasted seven days, which is a complete period, tells us that this is to last throughout our whole sojourn on earth.

It is to this that Paul referred when he stated: *"Purge out therefore the old leaven, that you may be a new lump, as you are unleavened. For even Christ our Passover is sacrificed for us: therefore let us keep the feast, not with old leaven, neither with the leaven of malice and wickedness; but with the unleavened bread of sincerity and truth"* (I Cor. 5:7-8).

All of this was a type as it regarded Old Testament means and methods; however, it was meant to portray that which Christ would do within our hearts and lives.

Every Christian knows that all sin must be purged out of our lives; however, the great question is, how is this done? If we miss it here, then we miss it altogether.

THE CROSS

Once again, we go back to the Cross. Remember that Paul said, *"For even Christ our passover is sacrificed for us"* (I Cor. 5:7).

While the Scripture doesn't teach sinless perfection, it definitely does teach that sin shall not have dominion over us, and this basically speaks of the sin nature (Rom. 6:14).

There is only one way that the child of God can walk in victory—not five ways, three ways, or even two ways—only one. We go back to the original meaning in the text in Exodus, Chapter 13, as it speaks of Christ.

The church has run aground in 10,000 different ways in attempting to carry out this of which we speak, and I refer to living an overcoming, Christian life. It can only be done in Christ, but how is it done in Christ?

The clue is in what Paul said concerning Christ's sacrifice of Himself (I Cor. 5:7). As the second man, i.e., the representative man (I Cor. 15:45-50), which refers to Christ being our substitute, He has done all things for us simply because it was impossible for us to do them ourselves.

In other words, if man were to be saved, salvation would wholly have to come from outside of man, which it did in the realm of Christ and the Cross. While everything Christ did played a great part in the redemption process, the believer must first of all zero in on the sacrifice of Christ, even as Paul stated, that is, if he is to understand redemption.

As is obvious, this refers to the Cross.

ALL IS MADE POSSIBLE BY
CHRIST AND THE CROSS

As a believer, we must understand that every single thing we have from the Lord, irrespective as to what it might be, has been made possible by what Christ did at the Cross. That must be the foundation of believing—the foundation of our faith.

Having anchored our faith in the sacrifice of Christ, which means we have made the Cross of Christ the object of our faith, the Holy Spirit, who is the key to all of our victory, can then function and work unhindered within our hearts and lives (Rom. 6:3-5, 10-14; 8:1-11).

Far too often we attempt to rid ourselves of sin by man-devised rules and regulations, which, in fact, the Holy Spirit will never honor. In other words, unless the Holy Spirit works within us, which He, of course, desires to do, we will be left functioning within the capacity of our own personal strength. We will quickly find this to be woefully insufficient.

To get you started, which I've already stated any number of times in this volume, always understand that Christ gives us all things through what He did at the Cross. Consequently, our faith must rest in that finished work, which then gives the Holy Spirit latitude to work unhindered within our lives. As stated, I have said this over and over and will continue to say it throughout this volume because it's so very, very important.

The Holy Spirit works entirely within the parameters of the sacrifice of Christ, meaning that it is the Cross that gives the Holy Spirit the legal means to do all that He does.

That's why Paul said: *"For the law of the Spirit of life in Christ Jesus has made me free from the law of sin and death"* (Rom. 8:2).

A SIGN

"And you shall show your son in that day, saying, This is done because of that which the LORD did unto me when I came forth out of Egypt. And it shall be for a sign unto you upon your hand, and for a memorial between your eyes, that the LORD's law may be in your mouth: for with a strong hand has the LORD brought you out of Egypt. You shall therefore keep this ordinance in his season from year to year" (Ex. 13:8-10).

The great things that the Lord has done for us—and, to be sure, He has done many—must never be forgotten. They must be related over and over, and for a number of reasons:

- We must ever be mindful that it is the Lord who has done these things and not we ourselves.
- The relating to our children the great events done by the Lord builds faith in them that they might expect great and mighty things as well.
- All of this relates to an accomplished fact. The basis of this feast was what the Lord had done for Israel in delivering them from the land of bondage. In other words, its foundation was redemption accomplished,

entered into, known, and enjoyed. It speaks of a work already accomplished. Until this joy of assurance is ours, there cannot be any feasting upon Christ.

PHYLACTERIES

There can be little doubt that the Jewish system of phylacteries grew mainly out of this passage and was intended as a fulfillment of the commands contained in it.

These phylacteries that Jesus mentioned were strips of parchment (leather) with passages of Scripture written upon them and deposited in small boxes that were fastened by a strap either to the left arm or across the forehead.

The original intention by the Holy Spirit was according to the following: It was to be a sign upon the hand that signified that all service was consecrated to God.

It was also to be a *"memorial between the eyes,"* that is, upon the forehead, where all could see, which, being interpreted, signified an open manifestation of separation unto God.

Finally, it was to be accompanied with *"the Lord's law in their mouth,"* which meant that the law was ever to be the basis of all action taken.

Used in the right manner, it would be a great blessing to the people. As a front for self-righteousness, which happened with some, Jesus replied, *"But all their works they do for to be seen of men: they make broad their phylacteries, and enlarge the borders of their garments"* (Mat. 23:5).

The idea was, as is obvious, some in Jesus' day wore large phylacteries to make themselves seem spiritual to others. Our Lord condemned this and did so strongly.

From its original purpose, the Jews had come to believe—and we continue to speak of the time of Christ—that the wearing of these things warded off demon spirits; however, this was reducing the Word of God to mere superstition and some type of magic incantation.

CONFESSION OF SCRIPTURE

The modern confession of Scripture as enjoined by the Word of Faith practitioners comes perilously close to this condemned by Christ.

They teach that if a problem is encountered, one should find particular Scriptures that address that problem, whatever it might be, memorize them, and then quote them over and over.

This is supposed to stir the Holy Spirit into action in order for the problem to be addressed.

The memorizing and quoting of Scriptures is something that every believer ought to do, which will always be a great blessing if used correctly; however, if not used correctly, it will come out to the same result as the Jews of old—superstition.

The quoting of Scriptures over and over doesn't force God into action. Neither does it manipulate some type of force in the spirit world that brings forth positive results. Again we state that all of that is superstition, which God can never honor. The Word of God, in its true form, is always linked to the sacrifice of Christ. Unfortunately, the Word of Faith people have divorced the Word from its author, and the price that He paid (Jn. 1:1).

Everything we receive from the Lord comes to us through Christ and what He has done for us at the Cross. If we try to impose another way or method, we insult Christ and, therefore, do violence to the Word of God.

REDEMPTION

> *And it shall be when the* LORD *shall bring you into the land of Canaanites, as He swore unto you and to your fathers, and shall give it you, that you shall set apart unto the* LORD *all that opens the matrix, and every firstling that comes of a beast which you have; the males shall be the* LORD's. *And every firstling of an ass you shall redeem with a lamb; and if you will not redeem it, then you shall break his neck: and all the firstborn of man among your children shall you redeem. And it shall be when your son asks you in time to come, saying, What is this? that you shall say unto him, By strength of hand the* LORD *brought us out from Egypt, from the house of bondage* (Ex. 13:11-14).

Williams said, "Verse 13 legislated for the redemption of a man and of an ass by the death of a lamb. This is humbling to human pride. The ass was an unclean animal; and with its broken neck, fitly pictured the true moral condition of the most highly cultivated man. But the death of the lamb obtained redemption. Only thus can sinners be saved."

The mule is the most stupid and senseless creature. So also is the natural man. Proudly as he may boast of his powers of reason, and conceited as he may be over his intellectual achievements, the truth is, he is utterly devoid of any spiritual intelligence.

Pink says, "Again, the 'ass' is stubborn and intractable, so also is the natural man. The sinner is rebellious and defiant. He will not come to Christ that he might have life (Jn. 5:40). It is in view of these things that Scripture declares, 'For vain men would be wise, though man be born like a wild ass colt" (Job 11:12).

BY STRENGTH OF HAND

And it shall be when the LORD shall bring you into the land of Canaanites, as He swore unto you and to your fathers, and shall give it you, that you shall set apart unto the LORD all that opens the matrix, and every firstling that comes of a beast which you have; the males shall be the LORD's. And every firstling of an ass you shall redeem with a lamb; and if you will not redeem it, then you shall break his neck: and all the firstborn of man among your children shall you redeem. And it shall be when your son asks you in time to come, saying,

What is this? that you shall say unto him, By strength of hand the LORD brought us out from Egypt, from the house of bondage (Ex. 13:11-14).

Unredeemed man thinks very highly of himself; however, as we can see from these passages, the Lord puts him in the same category as a dumb mule or donkey.

In Verse 13, we find two classes—the clean and the unclean. Man is classed with the latter. The lamb was to answer for the unclean, and if the ass was not redeemed, its neck was to be broken.

So, an unredeemed man was put on the same level with an unclean animal, moreover, in a condition in which nothing could be more worthless and unsightly. What a humiliating picture of man in his natural condition!

MAN'S EMPTY BOASTING

The lamb is pictured as a clean animal because it typifies Christ. In essence, Christ was the Lamb—the clean, the spotless Lamb. We were unclean, but He took our position, and on the Cross was made sin and treated as such. That which we should have endured throughout the countless ages of eternity, He endured for us on the tree. There and then, He bore all that was due to us in order that we might forever enjoy what is due to Him. He got our deserts that we might get His. The clean took, for a time, the place of the unclean in order that the unclean might take forever the place of the clean. Thus, whereas by nature we are represented by the loathsome figure of an ass with its neck broken, by grace we are represented by a risen and glorified Christ in heaven. That is an amazing contrast!

It lays man's glory in the dust and magnifies the riches of redeeming love. It silences man's empty boasting and puts into his mouth a hymn of praise to God and the Lamb, which shall swell throughout the courts of heaven during the everlasting ages.

GRACE

Mackintosh said:

It is interesting to see that by nature we are ranked with an unclean animal; by grace we are associated with Christ, the spotless Lamb. There can be nothing lower than the place which belongs to us by nature: nothing higher than that which belongs to us by grace. Look for example at an ass with its neck broken; there is what an unredeemed man is worth. Look at 'the precious blood of Christ'; there is what a redeemed man is worth. 'Unto you who believe is the preciousness.' That is, all who are washed in the blood of the Lamb partake of Christ's preciousness. As He is 'a living stone,' we are 'living stones'; as He is 'a precious stone,' we are 'precious stones.' We get life and preciousness all from Him and in Him. We are as He is. Every stone in the edifice is precious, because purchased at no less a price than 'the blood of the Lamb.' May the people of God know more fully our place and privileges in Christ!

ALIVE WITH CHRIST

"Now if we be dead with Christ, we believe that we shall also live with Him" (Rom. 6:8). What did Paul mean by this wonderful statement?

First of all, we can only live with Him if we are in Christ. Otherwise, we are *"dead in trespasses and sins"* (Eph. 2:1). Outside of Christ is no life; in Christ is all life.

However, if we are to truly live with Christ, which means to enjoy all that He is, all that He has, and all that He has done, which speaks of a victorious, overcoming, Christian experience, we must first of all "be dead with Christ." What does that mean?

In this statement as given by the apostle, he is referring back to Romans 6:3-5. This speaks of Christ being crucified, buried, and then rising from the dead, all on our behalf.

When the believing sinner evidences faith in Christ, even though he understands very little about what is happening, God likens that particular individual as literally being in Christ when the Saviour died, in Christ when the Saviour was buried, and in Christ when the Saviour rose from the dead.

In other words, Christ died as our substitute, becoming in a sense what we were (bearing the penalty of our sin), that we might become what He is (II Cor. 5:21).

IN THE LIKENESS OF HIS RESURRECTION

The apostle plainly told us, *"For if we have been planted together in the likeness of His death, we shall be also in the likeness of His resurrection"* (Rom. 6:5). That, in essence, says the same thing as Verse 8, *"Now if we be dead with Christ, we believe that we shall also live with Him."*

As is obvious here, everything hinges on the Cross. This is how man is redeemed, which means that he is redeemed in no other way. The lamb in Verse 13 is a type of Christ and what He would do to redeem humanity by dying on the Cross.

However, we must understand, and graphically so, that we can have this resurrection life, which is the greatest gift that God ever gave anyone, providing we understand that it is predicated solely on Christ and what He did for us at the Cross. It is the Cross of Christ that makes this possible.

That's why Paul said, and I quote him again, *"For if we have been planted together in the likeness of His death, we shall be also in the likeness of His resurrection."*

Now, please understand, even though it has links to the coming resurrection, that's not exactly what Paul was talking about here.

He was speaking primarily of the life that we live now, calling it resurrection life, which is the greatest life there is.

THE FIRSTBORN

So, we find in Verses 11 through 13 of Exodus, Chapter

13, that several things are said:

- When the children of Israel finally arrived in Canaan, which was the Promised Land, they were to conduct themselves in a specific manner. Unfortunately, because of unbelief, it would take them approximately 40 years to get there.
- All the firstborn of both man and beast was to be dedicated to the Lord, and we speak of boy babies and male animals. The firstborn was to represent Christ.
- Whenever the first boy baby was born and the first born of an ass, as well, both were to be redeemed at birth by the parents offering up a lamb in sacrifice. As we've already stated, this portrays the fact that unredeemed man is worth no more than a dumb mule.
- If the animal was not redeemed by a lamb, or in other words, the owner had no lamb to offer, then by law, he was to break the neck of the newborn animal, thereby, killing it. This proclaimed the fact that unredeemed man is destined to die without God.

THE COMPARISON OF UNREDEEMED MAN AND THE DUMB ANIMAL

It is instructive to trace the various references of the "ass" in Scripture. The first mention of this animal is found in Genesis, Chapter 22. From it, we learn two things:

1. The Scripture says: *"Abraham rose up early in the morning, and saddled his ass"* (Gen. 22:3). As is

obvious, this means that this animal was not free. It was a beast of burden—*"saddled."* So too is the sinner—serving diverse lusts.

2. Abraham said to the young men with him and Isaac, *"Abide you here with the ass; and I and the lad will go yonder and worship"* (Gen. 22:5). This tells us that the animal could not accompany Abraham and Isaac to the place of worship, and neither can the sinner worship God.

In Genesis 49:14, we read, *"Issachar is a strong ass couching down between two burdens."* The sinner is heavily laden as well (Mat. 11:28).

We also find that God forbade His people to plow with an ox and an ass together (Deut. 22:10). This means that the sinner is shut out from the service of God.

FEARFULLY SOLEMN IS THIS

In I Samuel 9:3, we are told: *"And the asses of Kish Saul's father were lost,"* and though Saul and his servants sought long for them, they recovered them not. The sinner, too, is lost, away from God, and no human power can restore him.

In Jeremiah 22:19, we read, *"He shall be buried with the burial of an ass, drawn and cast forth beyond the gates of Jerusalem."*

Pink said, "Fearfully solemn is this."

The carcass of the ass was cast forth outside the gates of the Holy City.

So shall it be with every sinner who dies outside of Christ; he shall not enter the New Jerusalem, but be *"cast into the lake of fire."*

The final reference to the ass is found in Zechariah 9:9: "Rejoice greatly, O daughter of Zion; shout, O daughter of Jerusalem: behold, your King comes unto you: He is just, and having salvation; lowly, and riding upon an ass."

A most blessed contrast is this. Here we see the ass entering Jerusalem, but only so as it was beneath the controlling hand of the Lord Jesus! Here is the sinner's only hope—to submit to Christ!

ISHMAEL

In Genesis 16:12, we have a statement that is very pertinent in this connection, though its particular force is lost in most translations.

The revised version says, and correctly so, *"And he shall be a wild-ass man among men; his hand shall be against every man, and every man's hand against him."*

Those were the words of the Lord to Hagar. They were a prophecy concerning Ishmael. From Galatians, Chapter 4, we learn that Ishmael stands for the natural man as Isaac stands for the believer, the seed of promise. In full accord then, with all that we have said above, is this striking description of Sarah's firstborn.

Of course, we're speaking of Ishmael. He was a *"wild-ass man."*

The Bedouin Arabs are his descendants, and fully do they witness to the truth of this ancient prophecy. We find it in the religion of Islam.

However, solemn is it to find that here we have God's description of the natural man, and more solemn still is what we read of Ishmael in Galatians, Chapter 4—he *"persecuted him who was born after the Spirit"* and, in consequence, had to be *"cast out"* (Gal. 4:29-30).

So, in effect, God classifies the religion of Islam as bogus, a religion of the flesh, and is held by *"wild-ass men."* Biblically, that's a very apt description.

DELIVERANCE

"And it came to pass, when Pharaoh would hardly let us go, that the LORD slew all the firstborn in the land of Egypt, both the firstborn of man, and the firstborn of beast: therefore I sacrifice to the LORD all that opens the matrix, being males; but all the firstborn of my children I redeem. And it shall be for a token upon your hand, and for front-lets between your eyes: for by strength of hand the LORD brought us forth out of Egypt" (Ex. 13:15-16).

These admonitions were given in order that in the days of their prosperity, the children of Israel would never forget the manner of their redemption. What do we mean by that statement?

Prosperity has a subtle influence in leading away the heart from God.

This danger is one to be jealously watched against.

Man's firstborn is a type of the firstborn of God, in His authority and priestly function among His brethren, and as the object of the Father's love and trust. In both Egypt's and Israel's firstborn, we find the twofold type of Christ and His people.

Egypt's firstborn died; Israel's were saved. The death of Egypt's firstborn burst the bonds of Israel; the death of God's firstborn, the bonds of His people.

THE CROSS

So, the Cross has a double effect: it condemns the Christ-rejecter, and it brings to salvation the Christ-acceptor.

This was to ever be kept before the children of Israel by the sacrifice of a lamb offered up at the time of the firstborn child, a male.

The phrase, *"But all the firstborn of my children I redeem,"* could be translated, "But all the firstborn of My children I redeem by My firstborn, who is Christ."

None of this means that the firstborns were automatically saved by virtue of their being born first. They were merely to serve as a type of Christ.

The token was the phylacteries that we have already mentioned, which were to be prominent on the left wrist and on the head between the eyes.

As we've already stated, the whole idea of all of this was that Israel not forget how she was delivered.

We should let that be a lesson to us that we not forget the Cross. It must ever be paramount in our doing and in our seeing.

Israel celebrated her deliverance by the keeping of the Passover: We celebrate our deliverance by the keeping of the Lord's Supper, which is an outgrowth of the Passover.

The difference is, the first was a type of the One who was to come, while the latter is a celebration of the One who has come, namely Christ.

THE LEADING OF THE LORD

"And it came to pass, when Pharaoh had let the people go, that God led them not through the way of the land of the Philistines, although that was near; for God said, Lest peradventure the people repent when they see war, and they return to Egypt" (Ex. 13:17).

We learn from this passage that God was leading Israel exactly as He desires to lead us presently. They were His people, so He would lead them.

How much does the average Christian seek the Lord as it concerns His leading and guidance?

We know from the Word of God that the Lord desires to lead us, but we have to seek such leading and not take it for granted (Jer. 33:3). In fact, we should pray about everything and ask the Lord for His will in all things.

To be sure, the Lord will definitely answer that type of prayer (Mat. 21:22; Mk. 11:24-25; Jn. 14:14; 15:7).

THE WAY THE LORD LEADS

As well, the Lord would lead Israel in a way that they would not normally go. If one looks at a map, one can see that the nearest route between Egypt and the land of Israel, then known as Canaan, is by the Mediterranean Sea. However, by going this route, before long, they would have run into the Philistines, who were a war-like people, which the Lord knew would be disconcerting to the children of Israel. In other words, their faith wasn't yet up to this level, and the Lord does not take us beyond our faith. He said, *"Lest peradventure the people repent when they see war, and they return to Egypt."*

As a new convert, the Lord is very jealous over us, and leads and directs us minutely; however, He expects us to grow in grace and the knowledge of the Lord. Please understand that the Lord is developing us, and, as well, Satan is ever present to hinder that development. To follow Christ means that we understand that all we have from Him comes to us through Christ and what Christ did at the Cross. If we follow the Lord as we should follow Him and place our faith in the Cross, ever making it the object of our faith, the Holy Spirit, to be sure, will see us through.

ORDER

"But God led the people about, through the way of the wilderness of the Red Sea: and the children of Israel went

up harnessed out of the land of Egypt" (Ex. 13:18).

This tells us that Israel's departure from Egypt was not a disorderly rout, but rather an orderly departure. God is never the author of confusion.

The word *harnessed* could be translated, "the children of Israel went up by five in a rank out of the land of Egypt." The fact that Israel went forth by five in a rank exemplified and expressed God's grace, for five in Scripture ever speaks of grace or favor. This probably refers to five large groups.

As well, when they went out of Egypt, even though it is not given in this account, the psalmist said, *"There was not one feeble person among their tribes"* (Ps. 105:37).

If there was ever a miracle, this was a miracle! Not a single one in all of that vast host was sickly or infirmed, irrespective of their ages.

In fact, the entirety of that verse says, *"He brought them forth also with silver and gold: and there was not one feeble person among their tribes."*

What does this mean to us presently? Does it mean that every believer ought to be wealthy and healthy?

In a sense, I definitely believe that it can mean that and, in fact, does mean that.

The deliverance of the children of Israel out of Egyptian bondage has a double meaning.

1. It refers to our salvation experience.
2. As well, it refers to the believer being led out of bondage into freedom, which means that he understands that Jesus is the source, while the Cross is the means.

Consequently, he can now have victory over the world, the flesh, and the Devil. It is definitely not God's will for anyone of His children to be ruled by the sin nature. It is God's will that we all walk in victory, and that means a perpetual victory. While the Bible does not teach sinless perfection, it most definitely does teach that *"sin* (the sin nature) *shall not have dominion over you"* (Rom. 6:14).

GOD'S PRESCRIBED ORDER OF VICTORY

Let me give you an abbreviated diagram of what this Message of the Cross is all about. Read each line closely and, as well, even each word.

- Jesus Christ is the source of all things we receive from God (Jn. 1:14; Rom. 6:1-14).
- The Cross of Christ is the means by which all of these things are made available to us (I Cor. 1:17, 18, 23; 2:2).
- Christ and Him crucified must without fail be the object of our faith, and the only object of our faith (Col. 2:10-15; Gal. 6:14).
- With Christ as our source, the Cross as our means, and our faith properly placed and maintained in Christ and the Cross, the Holy Spirit who works exclusively within the parameters, so to speak, of the finished work of Christ, i.e., the Cross, will grandly help us to live this life, and to do so victoriously.

WEALTH AND HEALTH

Wealth and health certainly were not the purpose of the children of Israel being delivered out of Egyptian bondage, but it was rather their being brought out from under the iron yoke of Pharaoh, who was a type of the Devil, and to whom they actually belonged as slaves. Still, health and wealth were given to the children of Israel even though it was not the prime purpose of their deliverance.

It is the same presently: Our salvation is being brought from unrighteousness to righteousness, from darkness to light, and from Satan to Christ. Of course, this is the central purpose and theme of redemption, and we must never forget that. As well, we must ever place the preeminence in Christ and the Cross, even as Israel was to do as it regarded the yearly keeping of the Passover.

IT IS PERFECTLY PROPER

By making certain that we keep our priorities right, it is perfectly proper, and even scriptural, that we believe God for finances as well as health, etc. We have a whole salvation. This means that we are saved spiritually, physically, financially, and mentally, but it doesn't mean that the believer will never sin again, that we will never be sick, or that we won't have financial difficulties at times. Sometimes we erroneously attempt to push the coming kingdom age into the present, which, of course, is unscriptural.

However, having said that, the Lord will do great and mighty things for anyone who will dare to believe Him.

When it comes to finances, we had best check our motives. Why do we want to be blessed? I realize that all of us instantly retort by saying that we want blessings for the work of God.

That is an excellent reason; however, the truth is, when many are blessed financially, they find it very difficult to bless the Lord's work. Money does strange things to people. Some few will walk before the Lord in all righteousness and holiness and will, therefore, do exactly what God wants them to do, but sadly, many do not fall into that category. They find it easy to give to the Lord when their tithes constitute $30 to $40 a week, but they find it very difficult when God blesses them, and their tithes should be $2,000 or $3,000 a week. That's the reason that the Lord finds it difficult to bless a lot of Christians. The truth is, He cannot trust them to do right.

THE WILDERNESS

There were many reasons that the Lord led the children of Israel by the way of the wilderness.

- The Egyptians would be drowned in their attempt to cross the Red Sea, which the Israelites had just crossed on dry ground. So, the Lord would rid Israel of her primary enemy, and do so in one fell swoop.
- The Lord would teach Israel faith and trust in the wilderness. In fact, the wilderness was such that whatever it was that was supplied to Israel, as it

regarded their sustenance and maintenance, would have to be provided by the Lord. It was a most inhospitable place, but the Lord would show them that He was able to set a table, so to speak, even in the wilderness, and for some 3 million souls at that!

WHAT WE LEARN FROM THE WILDERNESS EXPERIENCE

All of us want blessings, and rightly so; however, while we learn great things about God from blessings, the truth is, we learn next to nothing about ourselves. It is through adversity, and I continue to speak of the wilderness experience, that we learn about ourselves. How do we react? What does it take to reduce us to grumbling and complaining?

While the Lord is the great blesser, the truth is, He tempers His blessings with adversity. He is training the whole man, and I speak of how we should act toward God during times of blessings, and how we should react as it regards adversity.

So, the Lord would teach Israel much in the wilderness; however, the sadness is, they didn't come out too well.

JOSEPH

"And Moses took the bones of Joseph with him: for he had straitly sworn the children of Israel, saying, God will surely visit you; and you shall carry up my bones away *hence with you"* (Ex. 13:19).

Joseph was 110 years old when he died. He had been the vice-regent of Egypt for a number of years, actually saving that nation from starvation, plus saving surrounding nations as well. In effect, he had possibly been the second most powerful man in the world. However, even though he had the glory of Egypt given to him by God, his heart was never in Egypt but in Canaanland. That was the land promised to Abraham by God, where a mighty nation would rise up—a nation totally different than any other nation in the world, a people who belonged exclusively to Jehovah.

Joseph knew by revelation that a day was coming that God would deliver the children of Israel out of the land of Egypt. In fact, they were few when Joseph died, possibly several thousands at the most. As well, up until the time of his death, and even sometime afterward, they were treated royally by Pharaoh.

GOD WILL SURELY VISIT YOU

However, another Pharaoh ultimately arose who did not recognize Joseph, which was probably after Joseph died. Consequently, he made slaves of the children of Israel. Irrespective of all of this, Joseph knew by revelation from the Lord that God was going to deliver the children of Israel out of this land and take them to Canaan. Consequently, he gave explicit instructions that when this time would come—as most surely it would—his embalmed body, which, no doubt, was deposited in a mummy case, would be taken to Canaan as well.

All of this was evidently known among the Israelites because Moses was very careful to carry out this request. So, when they did quit Egypt, somewhere in that possession was the embalmed body of a man of faith, a man who had been the most beautiful type of Christ found in the entirety of the Old Testament. His body had probably been deposited at Tanis, which was the capital of the shepherd kings, from which it was now retrieved.

As well, there is some small evidence in the text that not only was the body of Joseph brought out but, also, the bodies of all the sons of Jacob. There is no reason they would not have given the same instructions. If, in fact, that did happen, to be sure, they would have been brought out as well.

Joseph had said, *"God will surely visit you; and you shall carry up my bones away hence with you,"* which they did!

RESURRECTION

Not so very long from now, there's going to be another exodus. Jesus referred to it as *"the resurrection of the just"* (Lk. 14:14). Paul called it *"a better resurrection"* (Heb. 11:35). John called it *"the first resurrection"* (Rev. 20:5).

At that coming time, which could happen at any hour, the sacred dust of every saint of God who has ever lived and died will be raised. God knows where every molecule is, which will be made into a glorified body that will join with the soul and the spirit that is now with Christ. Paul said: *"But God gives it a body as it has pleased Him, and to every seed his own body"* (I Cor. 15:38).

THE FIRST RESURRECTION

In this first resurrection, which Jesus guaranteed by His resurrection from the dead, every saint of God who has ever lived will take part. As well, all on earth who are alive at that moment, and who are in Christ, shall experience this glorious resurrection.

Paul said:

> *For this we say unto you by the word of the Lord, that we which are alive and remain unto the coming of the Lord* (the resurrection) *shall not prevent them which are asleep* (the saints of God who have died in the past, which includes all). *For the Lord Himself shall descend from heaven with a shout, with the voice of the archangel, and with the trump of God: and the dead in Christ shall rise first: Then we which are alive and remain shall be caught up together with them in the clouds, to meet the Lord in the air: and so shall we ever be with the Lord* (I Thess. 4:15-17).

Paul also said: *"Behold, I show you a mystery; we shall not all sleep* (some saints will be alive at that time), *but we shall all be changed, in a moment, in the twinkling of an eye, at the last trump: for the trumpet shall sound,*

> *and the dead shall be raised incorruptible, and we shall be changed* (I Cor. 15:51-52).

THE GLORY

As well, the words *rapture* and *resurrection* both speak of the same event. In other words, at this time, the rapture of the church, the Lord will not come all the way to the earth as He will at the second coming. In fact, at the first coming, He will come for the saints, and at the second coming, He will come with the saints.

GLORY OF THE SAINTS

Also, the glory of the saints will be different. In other words, as should be obvious, some saints live godlier lives than others.

In fact, many have given their lives for the cause of Christ. Concerning this glory, which will be forever and forever, Paul also said:

"There is one glory of the sun, and anther glory of the moon, and another glory of the stars: for one star differs from another star in glory. So also is the resurrection of the dead," and we might add, *"the sainted dead"* (I Cor. 15:41-42).

Here he plainly tells us that some will have more glory than others, with the measurement, no doubt, being faithfulness (Mat. 25:21).

THE EDGE OF THE WILDERNESS

"And they took their journey from Succoth, and encamped in Etham, in the edge of the wilderness" (Ex. 13:20).

Succoth means "booths" or "tents." This spoke plainly of the pilgrim character of the journey that lay before them. This was one of the great lessons learned by the first pilgrims: *"Here have we no continuing city"* (Heb. 13:14), for *"by faith he sojourned in the Land of Promise, as in a strange country, dwelling in tabernacles* (tents) *with Isaac and Jacob, the heirs with him of the same promise"* (Heb. 11:9).

In fact, booths are all that we have down here, for *"our conversation* (citizenship) *is in heaven"* (Phil. 3:20).

However, as just stated, the day is now near at hand when we shall exchange our temporary tents for the eternal mansions of the Father's house, for *"as we have borne the image of the earthy, we shall also bear the image of the heavenly"* (I Cor. 15:49).

A MIXED MULTITUDE

Back in Exodus 12:38, it says that *"a mixed multitude went up also with them."*

Concerning this, Pink said:

It has been well said that when a movement of God takes place, men are wrought upon by other motives than those by which the Holy Spirit stirs the renewed heart, and a mass of such attach themselves to those who are led forth. Witness the fact that when God called Abraham alone (Isa. 51:2), Terah (his father) and Lot (his nephew) accompanied him (Gen. 11:31). Witness the Gibeonites making a league with Joshua (Josh., Chpt. 9). So, too, we find that after the Jewish remnant returned from the captivity 'a mixed multitude' joined themselves to Israel (Neh. 5:17), though later 'they separated from Israel all the mixed multitudes' (Neh. 13:3). So, too, we read of the Pharisees and Sadducees coming to John the Baptist (Mat. 3:7)!

Pink went on to say, "The ungodly among the congregation of the Lord has been the great bane of God's saints in every age, the source of our weakness, and the occasion of much of our failure. It is because of this the Spirit of God says, 'Wherefore come out from among them and be ye separate'" (II Cor. 6:17).

The children of Israel were about to go into the wilderness; however, something would now happen that would be grand and glorious. The Lord never asks us to do anything but that He always goes with us for the express purpose of teaching and leading us and, as well, to guarantee our success.

THE PILLAR

"And the LORD went before them by day in a pillar of a cloud, to lead them the way; and by night in a pillar of fire,

*to give them light; to go by day and night: He took not away
the pillar of the cloud by day, nor the pillar of fire by night,
from before the people"* (Ex. 13:21-22).

Mackintosh said: "The Lord not only conducted them
safely outside the bounds of Egypt, but He also came down,
as it were, in His traveling chariot, to be their companion
through all the vicissitudes of their wilderness journey. This
was divine grace. They were not merely delivered out of the
furnace of Egypt and then allowed to make the best of their
way to Canaan—such was not God's manner toward them."

He went on to say, "He went before them. He was 'a guide,
a glory, a defense, to save them from every fear.'"

If the Lord went into the wilderness with them, and it is
plainly clear here that He did, then it is for certain that He
would see them through the wilderness and, thereby, bring
them out of the wilderness.

THE TRINITY

We see in all of this a perfect portrayal of the Trinity.

It was God the Father, as we would refer to Him now, who
heard the groanings of Israel, and who raised up a deliverer
for them.

The lamb without spot or blemish that was slain, with its
blood applied, which secured protection and deliverance,
typified God the Son. Understanding that, we must come to
the conclusion, as well, that the pillar of cloud given to Israel
for their guidance speaks to us of God the Holy Spirit. In

fact, at every point in all of this, we anticipate the teaching of the New Testament, in other words, the fulfillment of all these things in Christ, which were only anticipated in the Old Testament.

It would seem in Verses 21 and 22 that there were two distinct appearances; however, Exodus 14:24 proclaims *"the pillar of fire and of the cloud"* as just one pillar. It was the visible sign of the Lord's presence with Israel. It seems that its upper portion rose up to heaven in the form of a column, with its lower being spread out cloudwise over Israel's camp. It seems to have been a pillar of fire in its upper portion and a cloud below. As stated, the cloud typified the Holy Spirit.

Let's look at this as it's carried out in the Word of God and see how it speaks to us presently.

THE CROSS MUST BE FIRST

Israel was delivered by the death of the paschal lamb, with its blood being applied to the doorposts. Then the cloud was given. This is the order of the New Testament.

Jesus died on the Cross in order for man to be redeemed, rose from the dead, ascended on high, and then the Holy Spirit was sent back on the Day of Pentecost. As well, this is the manner of the Christian experience.

The sinner comes to Christ, is redeemed by the blood of the Lamb, and then the Holy Spirit comes to indwell the soul. However, His coming is always on the grounds of Christ's shed blood and the believer's faith in that atoning work. It is never because of any moral fitness or merit in us.

It is beautifully amazing that the great doctrinal treatment of the redemption plan in Romans follows this guideline minutely.

Pink said: "It is not until after the believing sinner is 'justified' (Rom. 5:1) that we read of the Spirit of God. In 2:4-10 we get repentance; in 3:22-28, faith; and then in 5:5 we read 'The love of God is shed abroad in our hearts by the Holy Spirit which is given unto us!'"

A GIFT TO THE CHILDREN OF ISRAEL

As should be obvious, the children of Israel had absolutely no idea as to the manifestation that the Lord would bring forth as it regarded the pillar of fire and the cloud. This was solely a gift of God, but let the reader understand this: Israel was now delivered from Egyptian bondage and, as stated, delivered through and by the shed blood of the lamb. As a result of what had happened, the gifts of God would now start flowing freely.

Peter said, *"Repent, and be baptized every one of you in the name of Jesus Christ for the remission of sins* (the Greek says, 'be baptized because your sins have already been remitted'), *and you shall receive the gift of the Holy Spirit"* (Acts 2:38).

Before His crucifixion, resurrection, and ascension, Jesus told His disciples that He would send them another Comforter. There is no hint that any of the apostles requested such because, at the time, they had no knowledge of such, even as the children of Israel had no knowledge of what God would do as it regarded the cloud.

This great gift as promised by our Lord was altogether on the part of Christ and the Father (Jn. 14:16).

THE CLOUD SERVED AS A GUIDE

"The LORD *went before them by day in a pillar of a cloud, to lead them the way; and by night in a pillar of fire"* (Ex. 13:21).

The Holy Spirit is given to us as our Lord said, *"To guide us into all truth"* (Jn. 16:13). If we are truly children of God, at the same time, we will be *"led by the Spirit of God"* (Rom. 8:14).

If there were other people in the wilderness, which there probably weren't, but still, if so, and they would have looked down from the heights on this encampment of Israel, they would have seen a strange sight.

The tabernacle was where God dwelt between the mercy seat and the cherubim. Hovering over that tabernacle by day was the cloud, and hovering over it at night was the pillar of fire. That would have been a strange sight to anyone who was not a follower of Jehovah.

The truth is, the children of Israel were being shepherded by the Holy Spirit, which meant that God was with them both day and night the entire distance. There was no reason for them to complain about anything considering that the One who made the heavens and the earth was traveling as their leader.

Isn't it the same presently? Why should we ever complain? Why should we ever question the Lord? Why should we ever doubt?

The Lord lives within us, which means that the Holy Spirit is with us 24 hours a day, seven days a week. We should ever be mindful of that in our conduct.

THE CLOUD WAS LIGHT

This speaks not only of visibility but, as well, of spiritual illumination. Many hundreds of years after this great episode of the deliverance of the children of Israel, Nehemiah said, *"You led them in the day by a cloudy pillar; and in the night by a pillar of fire, to give them light in the way wherein they should go"* (Neh. 9:12).

As Israel was led both day and night by this particular cloud, likewise, the Holy Spirit is to the believer, *"the Spirit of wisdom and understanding, the Spirit of counsel and might, the Spirit of knowledge and of the fear of the LORD"* (Isa. 11:2).

THE CLOUD WAS A COVERING

The psalmist said, *"He spread a cloud for a covering"* (Ps. 105:39).

The covering of which the psalmist spoke had less to do

with physical covering than it did protection.

Unfortunately, there are many in the modern church who look to man for covering instead of the Lord. Such a position is disastrous to say the least.

Paul said that we owe civil authorities obedience, that is, if what they demand does not violate the Word of God; however, when it comes to fellow Christians, we do not owe them the same obedience as we do civil authorities. In fact, as Paul laid down the guidelines by the Spirit in Romans 13:1-7, as it regarded submission to civil authority, he then said as it regarded fellow Christians, *"Owe no man anything, but to love one another: for he who loves another has fulfilled the law"* (Rom. 13:8).

While I love all brothers and sisters in the Lord, no man is my covering; that can only come from the Lord.

GOD SPOKE FROM THE CLOUD

The psalmist also said, *"He spoke unto them in the cloudy pillar"* (Ps. 99:7).

Concerning this, the psalmist was, no doubt, referring to the following passage, *"And it came to pass, as Moses entered into the tabernacle, the cloudy pillar descended, and stood at the door of the tabernacle, and the LORD talked with Moses"* (Ex. 33:9).

Presently, in fact, ever since the Day of Pentecost, the Holy Spirit has been, and is, the spokesman for the Holy Trinity.

Jesus said, *"He who has an ear, let him hear what the*

Spirit says unto the churches" (Rev., Chpts. 2-3).

To be sure, whatever the Holy Spirit speaks to us as believers will always and without exception coincide with the Word of God. If it deviates from the Word in any capacity, then it's simply not the Spirit speaking.

Concerning the cloud, Exodus 14:20 says, *"And it came between the camp of the Egyptians and the camp of Israel; and it was a cloud and darkness to them."*

In other words, what was a great blessing to Israel was a great hindrance to the Egyptians and was meant to be so.

Jesus said, *"I thank You, O Father, Lord of heaven and earth, because You have hid these things from the wise and prudent"* (Mat. 11:25).

It is said of the Holy Spirit, *"The Spirit of truth whom the world cannot receive"* (Jn. 14:17).

THE CLOUD RESTED UPON THE TABERNACLE

When Moses finished the work of building the tabernacle, the Scripture says: *"Then a cloud covered the tent of the congregation, and the glory of the* LORD *filled the tabernacle. And Moses was not able to enter into the tent of the congregation, because the cloud abode thereon, and the glory of the* LORD *filled the tabernacle"* (Ex. 40:33-35).

The tabernacle was a type of Christ. In fact, everything in this structure pointed to Christ.

Jesus said, *"The Spirit of the Lord is upon Me, because He has anointed Me"* (Lk. 4:18).

John said of Christ, *"I indeed baptize you with water unto repentance: but He who comes after me is mightier than I, whose shoes I am not worthy to bear: He shall baptize you with the Holy Spirit, and with fire"* (Mat. 3:11).

Every single thing we receive from the Lord as believers comes exclusively through Christ, and more particularly, what Christ did at the Cross. In fact, the Holy Spirit works exclusively within the parameters of the finished work of Christ (Jn. 14:17).

As well, Paul said concerning the Holy Spirit, *"For the law of the Spirit of life in Christ Jesus has made me free from the law of sin and death"* (Rom. 8:2).

The believer can have everything for which Christ paid such a price, but only if his faith is exclusively in Christ and what Christ has done at the Cross (Gal. 5:5-6).

IN THE WILDERNESS, THE CLOUD NEVER LEFT ISRAEL

Nehemiah said, *"Yet You in Your manifold mercies forsook them not in the wilderness: the pillar of the cloud departed not from them"* (Neh. 9:19).

Despite the many failures of Israel, the Lord never withdrew the cloudy pillar. It rested over the tabernacle, and when the temple was built, it rested in the Holy of Holies.

The Scripture says, *"And it came to pass, when the priests were come out of the Holy Place, that the cloud filled the house of the LORD"* (I Ki. 8:10).

The cloud only left when Israel, in essence, by her evil conduct, bade Him go. Even then, it was like He was extremely reluctant to leave.

The Scripture says: *"Then did the cherubims lift up their wings, and the wheels beside them; and the glory of the God of Israel was over them above. And the glory of the LORD went up from the midst of the city, and stood upon the mountain which is on the east side of the city"* (Ezek. 11:22-23).

THE SOON RETURN OF THE CLOUD

Thankfully, the Prophet Ezekiel also saw the cloud return. In fact, it has not happened yet, but it most definitely shall.

The prophet said: *"And, behold, the glory of the God of Israel came from the way of the east: and His voice was like a noise of many waters: and the earth shined with His glory. And it was according to the appearance of the vision which I saw, even according to the vision that I saw when I came to destroy the city"* (Ezek. 43:2-3).

This will be when the Lord has revealed Himself to Israel as it regards the second coming, and they have accepted Him as Lord, Saviour, and Messiah. He will then resume His covenant relationship with them, and then shall be fulfilled the ancient promise:

When the LORD shall have washed away the filth of the daughters of Zion, and shall have purged the blood of Jerusalem from the midst thereof by the spirit of judgment, and by the spirit of burning. And the LORD *will create upon every dwelling place of Mount Zion, and upon her assemblies, a cloud and smoke by day, and the shining of a flaming fire by night: for upon all the glory shall be a defense. And there shall be a tabernacle for a shadow in the daytime from the heat, and for a place of refuge, and for a covert from storm and from rain* (Isa. 4:4-6).

I look at the Cross upon Calvary,
And O what a wonder divine!
To think of the wealth it holds for me,
The riches of heaven are mine.

I find at the Cross blessed victory,
And grace for each step of the way;
The fount of God's love is flowing free,
And sweeter it grows day by day.

The Cross is my hope for eternity,
No merit have I of my own;
The shed blood of Christ my only plea,
My trust is in Jesus alone.

CHAPTER 4

FAITH AND UNBELIEF

FAITH AND UNBELIEF

"AND THE LORD SPOKE *unto Moses, saying, Speak unto the children of Israel, that they turn and encamp before Pi-hahiroth, between Migdol and the sea, over against Baal-zephon: before it shall you encamp by the sea*" (Ex. 14:1-2).

Williams said, "The fear, unbelief, and anger of the very people who had witnessed God's wonders in the land of Egypt, would appear incredible but that each Bible student finds these evils in his own heart, and learns by sad experience, that great depression of mind usually follows exceptional spiritual triumphs."

God would perform His greatest miracle in the very shadow of one of Egypt's chief gods.

Pharaoh would still try to stop Israel, in effect, brandishing his fists in the face of God. This time he would go too far and bring upon himself and his army swift destruction.

The Lord would now direct Israel to exactly where they should go. Up until now, it had been to the southeast.

Another day's journey in this direction would have taken them beyond the limits of Egypt, into the desert region east of the Bitter Lakes, which was dry, treeless, and waterless.

THE WAY OF THE LORD

In view of this, God changed the direction of their route from southeast to due south. This made them take a course by which the Bitter Lakes were placed on their left hand, and so they remained within the limits of Egypt.

This was a district that was fairly well watered but was shut off from the wilderness by the Bitter Lakes in the northern prolongation of the Gulf of Suez, with which they were connected.

This route was more suitable for them, providing water and some sustenance for the herds; however, it had one great drawback.

The drawback consisted of shutting them in-between their assailants should Egypt come after them, which they did. On the one hand was Egypt, and the sea was on the other. This circumstance seems to have led Pharaoh to make his pursuit.

THE GOD OF MIRACLES

From a military point of view, Israel had blundered badly. In effect, they were hemmed in; however, the following must be remembered: God was leading them, and, as well, He had a great plan and purpose for taking them on this particular route. He would rid them of Pharaoh and the Egyptian army once and for all.

In regard to this, we are to see one of the greatest miracles recorded in the Old Testament and, in fact, in the entirety of history. Actually, it was this notable event which made such a great impression upon the enemies of the Lord.

Rahab said: *"For we have heard how the LORD dried up the water of the Red Sea for you, when you came out of Egypt ... And as soon as we had heard these things, our hearts did melt, neither did there remain any more courage in any man, because of you: for the LORD your God, He is God in heaven above, and in earth beneath"* (Josh. 2:10-11).

The miracle of the Red Sea occupies the same place and position in the Old Testament as the resurrection of our Lord does in the New. It is appealed to as a standard of measurement as the supreme demonstration of God's power (Eph. 1:19).

FAITH AND UNBELIEF

Each generation of infidels and agnostics has directed special attacks against this miracle of the Red Sea crossing, but to the child of God, miracles occasion no difficulty.

Pink said, "The great difference between faith and unbelief is that one brings in God, and the other shuts Him out."

I want it stated unequivocally, clearly, and plainly that I am a believer. I believe in a God who can perform miracles, who performs miracles presently, and, in fact, has never stopped performing miracles, and greater still, will never stop performing miracles.

Jesus said, *"If you have faith as a grain of mustard seed, you shall say unto this mountain, Remove hence to yonder place; and it shall remove; and nothing shall be impossible unto you"* (Mat. 17:20).

Our Lord also said, *"If you can believe, all things are possible to him who believes"* (Mk. 9:23).

BAAL

It is believed that Baal-zephon was a shrine dedicated to Baal worship, in this case, referred to as "Typhon, the evil demon of Egyptian mythology." It is also believed that human sacrifices may have been offered here at this particular place.

At any rate, God would perform His greatest miracle in the very shadow of one of Egypt's chief gods. In fact, as should be overly obvious, all the things accomplished by the Lord would make the gods of Egypt look worthless by comparison, which they were.

The Lord had Israel to camp right in front of this worthless idol as if to say, "You claim to be so powerful; now is the time to show how powerful you really are!"

IDOL GODS

Nations of the world at that time worshipped particular idols, claiming them to be god. This means they were polytheistic. In fact, Israel was the only nation in the world at that time that was monotheistic, which means they worshipped only one God, that is, Jehovah.

We may think that the world presently has advanced far beyond such superstition, etc. However, in essence, if the Bible is not adhered to as it regards the worship of the Lord, which can only be done through His Son, the Lord Jesus Christ, in effect, men are then worshipping idols. These idols may go under the name of various religions, such as Hinduism, Buddhism, Shintoism, Islam, etc., but, in fact, demon spirits are behind these religions just as they were behind the idols of old.

SEDUCING SPIRITS

Unredeemed man may advance a little bit intellectually, but he cannot advance spiritually, not at all! So, even though he may have traded his idol, which he once fashioned with his hands, for that which seems to be more intellectual, the end result is the same—he is worshipping demons.

The same can be said for even parts of Christianity that have been perverted, which means it no longer adheres to the Word of God.

Concerning this, Paul said, "*Now the Spirit* (Holy Spirit) *speaks expressly, that in the latter times* (the times in which we now live) *some shall depart from the faith* (Jesus Christ and Him crucified), *giving heed to seducing spirits, and doctrines of devils* (demons)" (I Tim. 4:1).

This plainly tells us that demon spirits are behind all false doctrine— even referred to by Paul as doctrines of demons— and is unequivocally stating that these doctrines are fostered by seducing spirits.

This means that while it may sound like the Lord, may act like the Lord, and may even claim to be of the Lord, in fact, it is an *"angel of light"* producing these doctrines of demons (II Cor. 11:13-15).

THE CROSS

Please allow me to make a couple of strong statements: Unless the believer has a proper understanding of the Cross, he simply will not be able to understand the gospel or, in effect, the Word of God.

Listen again to Paul: *"For Christ sent me not to baptize, but to preach the Gospel: not with wisdom of words, lest the Cross of Christ should be made of none effect"* (I Cor. 1:17).

In effect, Paul says here that the Cross of Christ is the gospel. This refers to what Jesus did for us at the Cross, thereby, given to us by the Holy Spirit upon believing faith (Gal. 5:5-6). Paul is saying that the emphasis must never be on anything except Christ and the Cross, not even on water baptism, the Lord's Supper, etc.

While these things have their place and position and are important, still, it is the Cross of Christ where all emphasis must be placed.

That's why Paul also said, *"but we preach Christ crucified"* (I Cor. 1:23). He actually said that he preached Christ crucified, even though the Cross was a stumbling block to the Jews and *"unto the Greeks foolishness."*

So, if the preacher is not preaching the Cross, he is not preaching the gospel. If a person doesn't properly understand the Cross, then he cannot understand the gospel.

WHAT DOES IT MEAN TO PREACH THE CROSS?

Paul said, *"For the preaching of the Cross is to them who perish foolishness; but unto us who are saved it is the power of God."*

He then said, *"For after that in the wisdom of God the world by wisdom knew not God, it pleased God by the foolishness of preaching* (preaching the Cross) *to save them who believe"* (I Cor. 1:18, 21).

Sometime back, Frances handed me an advertisement for a book written by a prominent Word of Faith preacher. Someone had sent the magazine to us. The article plainly stated, and I quote him, "Whoever preaches the Cross preaches death." In other words, he was boldly repudiating the Cross and doing so in every capacity.

Sadly and regrettably, the Cross of Christ has no place in the Word of Faith doctrine, which has been accepted by great parts of the charismatic and Pentecostal worlds.

I do not mean to be unkind, but the truth is, the Word of Faith doctrine is a doctrine of demons and is perpetrated by seducing spirits. In fact, it just might be, and I personally believe is, the worst doctrine that Satan has ever perpetrated on the church.

It is grossly evil and has destroyed, is destroying, and shall destroy many, many people simply because it is carried out by those who claim to be Spirit-filled, and who claim to adhere to the Word of God.

THE EMPHASIS

The truth is, the main emphasis of this doctrine is not the atonement, and that's the reason that most of its followers are little aware of what it actually teaches about this subject. The main emphasis is money. In fact, that's the reason it draws so many adherents—the promise to be rich, etc. The sadness is, the only ones getting rich in this particular doctrine are the preachers.

The true biblical position of any doctrine must be the manner and the way in which it looks at the atonement. The atonement is the heart of the gospel. It's that for which Jesus died on Calvary, which refers to the manner in which people are saved, etc.

For instance, so-called Christian Science repudiates biblical atonement and is, therefore, false. Jehovah's Witnesses do the same. Modernism falls into the same category. In fact, the entirety of the Catholic Church places the atonement in the confines of the church instead of Christ. While Christ, in a sense, is proclaimed in that particular so-called faith, it is, in reality, another Jesus instead of the Christ of the Bible (II Cor. 11:4).

The Word of Faith doctrine falls into the category of the above simply because it has changed the atonement from the Cross of Christ to the confines of hell, of all places. Instead of it saying, "Jesus died on the Cross for you," it rather says, "Jesus went to hell for you." Now, think about that statement for a moment! The atonement is placed in the confines of hell, of all places. In other words, it teaches that while Jesus died on the Cross, that, in fact, "was a place of great defeat." In other words, this man, plus all adherents of the Word of Faith doctrine, teaches that there was no victory in the Cross.

All of this is very strange considering that Paul said, *"For the preaching of the Cross is to them who perish foolishness; but unto us who are saved it is the power of God"* (I Cor. 1:18).

Now, the preaching of the Cross and what Jesus did there is either the power of God, or else, it is a place of defeat. One cannot have it both ways. This means that you can believe what the Word of Faith preachers say, or you can believe what Paul said. As for me and my house, we'll take what Paul said.

Paul would hardly have preached the Cross had it been a place of defeat. No, it was the place of the greatest victory that mankind has ever known or shall know.

THE PRECIOUS BLOOD OF CHRIST

I'll tell you what it did by continuing to quote Paul:

"But now in Christ Jesus you who sometimes (in time past) *were far off are made nigh* (near) *by the blood of Christ"* (Eph. 2:13). This plainly tells us that our salvation is in the Cross, where Jesus shed His precious life's blood.

The Word of Faith teachers claim that while Jesus died on the Cross, this had nothing to do with our salvation and victory.

They claim that He became a sinner on the Cross, died as a sinner, and as a sinner, He went to hell, and we speak of the burning side of hell. They also claim that He burned in hell for some three days and nights and suffered the agony of the damned, with Satan thinking that he had now defeated Christ. At the end of the three days and nights, they claim that God said, "It is enough," and then Jesus was born again, as any sinner is born again, and raised from the dead.

Now, the truth is, all of this is made up out of whole cloth. In other words, it is a fabrication pure and simple, with not one shred of it being found in the Word of God.

They derive their interpretation, or at least a part of it, from a false interpretation of the word *firstborn*. It comes from the following Scripture where Paul said: *"For whom He* (God) *did foreknow, He also did predestinate to be conformed to the image of His Son, that He* (Jesus) *might be the firstborn among many brethren"* (Rom. 8:29).

THE FIRSTBORN

The word *firstborn* is the translation from the Greek word

prototokos. The Greek scholars tell us that there is no proper English word which suitably explains the word *prototokos*, with the word *firstborn* being the best that English does produce.

As it regards Paul's statement, it definitely doesn't mean that Jesus was born again, but rather it means that He was the founder of the great salvation plan.

Colossians 1:15 says concerning Christ, *"Who is the image of the invisible God, the firstborn of every creature."*

That doesn't mean that Jesus, as God, was created in the distant past. It rather means that He was the creator of all things (Jn. 1:1-3).

Likewise, it says of Christ, *"And He is the head of the body, the church: who is the beginning, the firstborn from the dead; that in all things He might have the preeminence"* (Col. 1:18).

The term *"firstborn from the dead,"* as it speaks here of Christ, refers to Him being the resurrection. In other words, what He did at the Cross in His resurrection makes the resurrection possible for all believers, which will shortly come to pass. So, the word *firstborn* doesn't mean that Jesus was born again as a sinner is born again, but rather that He is the founder of the great salvation plan, which, in effect, was made possible by the Cross.

PREACHING THE CROSS

Getting back to our original thought, preaching the Cross

doesn't mean that the preacher has to give the story of the Cross every time he preaches. It simply means that he understands and believes that the Cross of Christ is the foundation of all doctrine. It is there where Jesus effected our atonement. That means that our salvation was not effected or brought about by His resurrection, ascension, and exaltation, as necessary and significant as were all of these events. In fact, these events were made possible by what Jesus did at the Cross. All sin was atoned at the Cross and not in the resurrection. In fact, even if one sin had been left unatoned, the resurrection of Christ would have been impossible simply because *"the wages of sin is death"* (Rom. 6:23). However, with all sin atoned, Satan could not stop the resurrection of Christ. In fact, it was never in doubt.

Once again, notice Paul. He said, *"But God forbid that I should glory* (boast), *save in the Cross of our Lord Jesus Christ"* (Gal. 6:14). He didn't say, "But God forbid that I should glory, save in the resurrection of our Lord Jesus Christ"

It is definitely true that we are resurrection people; however, it is true only in respect to our understanding of the Cross.

Again Paul said, *"For if we have been planted together in the likeness of His death, we shall be also in the likeness of His resurrection"* (Rom. 6:5).

This means that we can have resurrection life only to the extent that we understand the *"likeness of His death."*

If the preacher of the gospel truly understands the Cross and, thereby, truly believes the Cross, he will make it the foundation of all his preaching, in effect, making it the center of all things. That doesn't mean that he'll preach about the Cross every time he preaches, etc., but does definitely mean that everything he does preach will be based on that sure foundation.

THE WILDERNESS

"For Pharaoh will say of the children of Israel, They are entangled in the land, the wilderness has shut them in" (Ex. 14:3).

Through foreknowledge, the Lord knew what Pharaoh would reckon in his evil heart when he saw the children of Israel seemingly hemmed in.

God knows all things—past, present, and future—and if we follow Him, no mistakes will be made. In other words, while He might lead us purposely into the wilderness, He will go with us, and to be sure, will stay with us and will bring us out. We must ever understand that every single thing He does with us, of us, for us, by us, and in us is all according to design and is meant to ever bring us nearer to Him, who is the source of all life.

It is not for us to understand all His ways; it is up to us to have faith in all His ways, whether we understand them or not.

The problem with man, and even with Christian man, is that he thinks he knows more than God, or at least he acts that way. To fully know the Lord is to fully love Him and to fully trust Him. When one is completely placed in the center of God's will, one will find the greatest security, the greatest assurance, the greatest joy, and the greatest fulfillment of life there could ever be.

That's why Jesus said, *"The thief* (Satan) *comes not, but for to steal, and to kill, and to destroy: I am come that they might have life, and that they might have it more abundantly"* (Jn. 10:10).

THE HARDENED HEART

"And I will harden Pharaoh's heart, that he shall follow after them; and I will be honored upon Pharaoh, and upon all his host; that the Egyptians may know that I am the LORD. *And they did so"* (Ex. 14:4).

The idea is that God would provide the means by which Pharaoh would harden his own heart. God is said to do many things when, in fact, He does not personally do such but does set the stage.

In fact, this situation, as it regards Pharaoh, is but an example of what is going on every hour of every day all over the world, and it has always functioned in this capacity. Everything that God does brings about a response from the hearts of men. They can either accept or reject. As we previously said, the sun hardens clay and softens wax. The sun doesn't change, but the response of the particular materials is different.

At this very moment, God is doing things all over the

world that are having a tendency to either cause people to rebel against God or to accept the Lord and His ways.

The will of man is never violated by God. The Scripture emphatically states, *"Whosoever will"* (Jn. 3:16; 7:37-38; Rom. 10:13; Rev. 22:17).

THE WILL OF MAN

In fact, God guards the will of man as it respects acceptance or rejection of Him, but that is the only aspect of the will that is so guarded by God. It applies to both the redeemed and the unredeemed.

Let us look first at the unredeemed: Show me an alcoholic who is in the last stages of that terrible bondage, who cannot—within his own strength and power—quit drinking. But yet, if that alcoholic, or whomever it might be, desires to accept Christ as the Holy Spirit moves upon him, he can do exactly that, and Satan cannot stop it. In the born-again experience, the Lord will set that captive free of all bondages.

Unfortunately, when it comes to the redeemed, most Christians have an erroneous concept of the will. In fact, most think that now that they have become a Christian, they are perfectly free to say either yes or no to sin. Consequently, they are taught that if one sins, and, of course, we're speaking of believers, then it's because he wants to do that, whatever it might be. None of that is correct!

The believer is perfectly free in his spirit and will to say yes to Jesus Christ and what Christ has done for him at the

Cross, which means to obey the Word and to be guided by the Holy Spirit (Jn. 16:13).

WILLPOWER

However, if the Christian attempts to overcome sin by his willpower, he will fail every time, meaning that Satan will actually override his will. Let's say it in a different way so there will be no misunderstanding.

Yes, if the believer is not looking fully to Christ and the Cross, which is the only answer for sin, Satan can override the believer's will, despite the fact that the Christian is trying to say no to sin. Trusting in one's own willpower means that one is trusting in self and not Christ and the Cross.

Listen to what Paul said: *"For I know that in me (that is, in my flesh,) dwells no good thing: for to will* (willpower) *is present with me; but how to perform that which is good I find not"* (Rom. 7:18).

Paul is plainly saying here that before he understood Christ and the Cross, he tried to live for God by his own strength and willpower. When he said, *"To will is present with me,"* he was actually saying that he was trying to say no to sin, but to no avail. By using the term, *"But how to perform that which is good I find not,"* he was saying that despite all of his strength and trying to say no to sin, he found himself failing just the same (Rom. 7:15).

That, regrettably, is the condition of most Christians simply because they do not know or understand God's prescribed order of victory. Unfortunately, due to a lack of proper teaching, this is where most Christians find themselves—trying to live for God by the means of willpower alone, which guarantees defeat.

GOD'S PRESCRIBED ORDER

As we've already stated any number of times, if the believer will understand that everything he receives from the Lord comes to him exclusively through Christ and what Christ did at the Cross, and he places his faith there and keeps his faith there, he will then find the Holy Spirit grandly working on his behalf, bringing about victory within his life.

The sadness is, as we have repeatedly stated, most Christians have been taught little or nothing about the Cross of Christ, and, in fact, many at this present time have actually been taught against the Cross. As we've already explained, the Word of Faith doctrine is probably the greatest culprit as it regards this terrible error, which brings defeat to so many Christians.

CONCUPISCENCE

Let's look at it closer. Paul said: *"But sin* (the sin, referring to the sin nature), *taking occasion by the commandment* (the law of Moses, the moral part, the Ten Commandments), *wrought in me all manner of concupiscence* (evil desire). *For without the law sin was dead"* (Rom. 7:8).

Concupiscence, as stated, means "passionate or evil desire." It can pertain to anything in the realm of evil. The sad thing is that not understanding the Cross of Christ, the majority of Christians are in the same proverbial boat as was the Apostle Paul before he understood the Cross as it regards concupiscence. In fact, there are millions of Christians at this very moment who are struggling with evil desires and are fighting with all of their strength and might, but sadly, they are losing that fight.

They don't understand why they are losing, considering that they are struggling against this thing, whatever it might be, with every ounce of strength they have. Some have even thought that they are demon possessed because of these terrible, evil desires.

No, you aren't demon possessed, and neither are you a unique case. Your problem is this: The Cross is God's answer to sin and, in fact, His only answer. Most Christians understand the Cross, at least up to a point, as it regards salvation; however, they understand it not at all as it regards sanctification. Whether the Christian understands it or not, it is sanctification of which we speak here.

SPIRITUAL ADULTERY

Sadly and regrettably, even as we've already stated, as it regards sanctification, in other words how we live for God on a daily basis, the Cross is either totally ignored, or else, it is repudiated as the answer. The latter of these falls into the Word of Faith camp. Either way, the believer is in trouble because if he tries to live a life of victory outside of faith in the Cross, it presents itself as unfaithfulness to Christ and, in fact, in the mind of God, such a person is looked at as a spiritual adulterer (Rom. 7:1-4).

In other words, any Christian that's trying to live a life of victory outside of faith in the Cross is being unfaithful to Christ. He may not realize that and, in fact, may not think of himself in that capacity and would probably vigorously deny such. However, the truth is, even as Paul explained it, whether he realizes it or not, he is living a life of spiritual unfaithfulness, which translates into spiritual adultery. He is looking to things other than Christ and Him crucified as the answer. As stated, he is being unfaithful to Christ, and such is labeled as spiritual adultery.

THE WAY THE HOLY SPIRIT WORKS

In such an atmosphere, the Holy Spirit will not work. In other words, He will not help you to live a victorious life when you are trying to rely upon your own strength and ability. If He helped you in such a capacity, He would be helping you to commit spiritual adultery, which, of course, He will never do.

As a believer, you have the help of the Holy Spirit as long as you work within the parameters of the finished work of Christ (Rom. 8:1-2, 11). If you try to work outside of those parameters, which most of the modern church does, you will do so on your own. This means the Holy Spirit will have no part in such a situation, which leaves you helpless. That's the reason that millions of Christians are struggling with concupiscence (evil desires). Despite trying to stop this problem, they are not only not succeeding in getting victory, but the situation is actually becoming worse.

The Holy Spirit works entirely within the confines, so to speak, of the finished work of Christ, i.e., the Cross. That's what gives Him the legal means to do all that He does (Rom. 8:2). He doesn't demand much of us, but He does demand one thing, and that is that the Cross of Christ, or one might say, Jesus Christ and Him crucified, ever be the object of our faith.

We must understand that Jesus Christ is the source of all things that we receive from God, and the Cross is the means by which all of this is done. With that being carried out, the Holy Spirit, who is God, will grandly help us to be what we ought to be. Otherwise, He is hindered greatly.

Considering that He can do anything, this is help that we desperately need.

THE WORKS OF THE FLESH

Paul outlined the works of the flesh in Galatians, Chapter 5:

"*Adultery, fornication, uncleanness, lasciviousness, idolatry, witchcraft, hatred, variance, emulations, wrath, strife, seditions, heresies, envyings, murders, drunkenness, revelings, and such like: of the which I tell you before, as*

I have also told you in time past, that they which do such things shall not inherit the kingdom of God" (Gal. 5:19-21).

If it is to be noticed, heresies fall under the category of *"works of the flesh."*

There are untold numbers of preachers and untold numbers of believers who are, in a sense, not guilty of the sin of concupiscence but are guilty of works of the flesh in other capacities.

For instance, heresies are listed as a work of the flesh. This means that any preacher who preaches erroneous doctrine, and any believer who believes such, are guilty of heresy.

HERESY

Heresy is a truth enlarged all out of proportion to its original intent. For instance, grace is certainly a great biblical doctrine; however, if people take grace into license—which many were doing in Paul's day and continue to do unto this hour—they have taken that truth into heresy.

Let me say it in another way: If the believer—preacher or otherwise—doesn't understand the Cross, in some way, irrespective of his efforts otherwise, works of the flesh are going to dominate his life in some manner. If it is to be noticed, these particular works cover the waterfront. In other words, just because a Christian is not committing the sins of adultery, fornication, drunkenness, etc., it doesn't necessarily mean that works of the flesh aren't being manifested. There are many categories as it regards this particular realm of sin.

FRUIT OF THE SPIRIT

In the same chapter, Paul refers to the fruit of the Spirit: *"love, joy, peace, longsuffering, gentleness, goodness, faith, meekness, temperance: against such there is no law"* (Gal. 5:22-23).

Now, let me make another statement as it regards the Cross. As it's impossible to overcome works of the flesh without properly understanding the Cross, likewise, it is impossible for the fruit of the Spirit to be developed in one's life unless one understands the Cross.

If it is to be noticed, it is fruit of the Spirit and not fruit of our own efforts, etc. In other words, the Holy Spirit alone can develop such fruit.

How does He do this?

Everything that is done in our lives as it regards the Lord is all done through the principle of faith. Paul said, *"For we through the Spirit wait for the hope of righteousness by faith."* He then said, *"For in Jesus Christ neither circumcision avails anything, nor uncircumcision; but faith which works by love"* (Gal. 5:5-6).

What does he mean by the use of the term *faith*?

Always and without exception, when Paul uses the term *faith*, or the term "in Christ" or one of its derivatives, he is speaking of the work of Christ on the Cross. In other words, we are to have faith in Christ and what Christ did for us at the Cross. This is the faith alone that God will honor, which overcomes the world.

If the believer properly understands the Cross, all the other attributes promised to the believer will be made available, but without that proper understanding, the Christian is greatly hindered in his spiritual progress. In fact, there can be precious little progress at all. We must ever understand that the message always has been, is, and ever shall be Jesus Christ and Him crucified (I Cor. 1:23).

PHARAOH'S LAST FLING

"And it was told the king of Egypt that the people fled: and the heart of Pharaoh and of his servants was turned against the people, and they said, Why have we done this, that we have let Israel go from serving us?" (Ex. 14:5).

Now begins the record of the greatest miracle to date, with the exception of creation itself. This miracle would be the opening of the Red Sea, which would be life to the Israelites and death to the Egyptians.

Egypt was extremely reluctant, to say the least, to give up hundreds of thousands of craftsmen, engineers, and laborers, who were such a boon to the Egyptian economy. Hence, they said, *"Why have we done this, that we have let Israel go from serving us?"*

What a fool man is!

Understanding that the Israelites were *"entangled in the land,"* they were *"shut in"* by the wilderness, and, as well, they were trapped before the Red Sea, did Pharaoh suppose that the God of miracles, who had acted so powerfully on behalf of Israel up till now, would simply let the tyrant destroy His people? God had already shown Himself exceedingly strong on Israel's behalf. Would not He continue to do so?

As stated, what a fool man is! Pharaoh had disregarded every warning. In the very face of God, he now marched out against Jehovah's redeemed to consume them in the wilderness, or so he thought.

In all the miracles performed by God in the last few weeks or months, Egypt's army had not been touched. Her chariots were intact, with her armies still the fighting force it had always been. So, Pharaoh evidently thought that his time of vengeance had now arrived.

Concerning this time, Mackintosh said, "It is when the people of God are brought into the greatest straits and difficulties that they are favored with the finest displays of God's character and actings; and for this reason He oftimes leads us into a trying position, in order that He may the more markedly show Himself."

THE PURSUIT

"And he made ready his chariot, and took his people with him: And he took six hundred chosen chariots, and all the chariots of Egypt, and captains over every one of them. And the LORD hardened the heart of Pharaoh king of Egypt, and he pursued after the children of Israel: and the children of Israel went out with a high hand. But the Egyptians pursued after them, all the horses and chariots

of Pharaoh, and his horsemen, and his army, and overtook them encamping by the sea, beside Pi-hahiroth, before Baal-zephon" (Ex. 14:6-9).

The 600 chosen chariots comprised the king's guard, the pride of Egypt. As well, all the other chariots of Egypt as the main body of the army, including the chariot drivers and combatants in each chariot, joined in with the king's guard. Josephus recorded that Pharaoh had 50,000 horsemen and 200,000 footmen, as well as all the chariots.

It is uncertain how long the Israelites remained encamped at Pi-hahiroth, but, to be sure, they waited as long as the pillar of cloud did not move (Num. 9:18-20).

It would have taken Pharaoh at least a day to hear of their march from Etham, at least another day, or perhaps even more, to collect his troops, and three or four days to effect the march from Tanis to Pi-hahiroth. The Jewish tradition is that the Red Sea was crossed on the night of the twenty-first of Nisan (Abib), which corresponds somewhat with our April.

Verse 8 says, *"The children of Israel went out with a high hand."* This refers to a certain degree of pride and confidence. Regrettably, the high hand would change when they faced the Red Sea.

THE MODERN CHURCH

Tragically, there are millions of Christians presently who unwillingly serve the Devil. It is a travesty because it doesn't' have to be this way. Whenever the believing sinner is born again, every bondage of Satan is broken, and that person no longer serves the Evil One. So, with that being the case, how is it that we can say there are millions of Christians who are, in fact, presently serving Satan?

As we've just stated, at the moment of conversion, every single sin is washed clean, with every bondage broken. In fact, God could not accept anyone on any other basis.

Concerning conversion, Paul said, *"You are washed ... You are sanctified ... You are justified in the name of the Lord Jesus, and by the Spirit of our God"* (I Cor. 6:11).

It is impossible for one to be justified without being made perfectly clean, which can only be done by the blood of Jesus and our faith in that finished work. In other words, there is no such thing as a partial justification. One is either justified, which means total and complete, or else, one is not justified, which means that one is still in one's sins.

So, as we've already asked, that being the case, how is it that millions of Christians are presently continuing to serve Satan?

Paul explained that to us in Romans, Chapters 6, 7, and 8.

ROMANS, CHAPTER SIX

In Romans, Chapter 6, he told us how that when Jesus was crucified, we were, in effect, *"baptized into His death"* (Rom. 6:3). We were then *"buried with Him by baptism into death,"* and then raised with Him *"in newness of life"* (Rom. 6:4).

This means that *"our old man was crucified with Him,"* which refers to all that we were before salvation. In other words, we died with Christ and, thereby, died to all of the things that once ensnared us.

That's the reason that Paul now speaks of the believer by saying, *"Therefore if any man be in Christ, he is a new creature: old things are passed away; behold, all things are become new"* (II Cor. 5:17).

As a result, *"the body of sin might be* (is) *destroyed, that henceforth we should not serve sin"* (Rom. 6:6). This means that the effectiveness of the sin nature is destroyed, with all bondages broken and guilt removed.

THE SIN NATURE

However, even though the Scripture plainly tells us that we are dead, having died in Christ, it doesn't say that the sin nature is dead, even though its power is broken.

It does say: *"Likewise reckon you also yourselves to be dead indeed unto sin* (the sin nature), *but alive unto God through Jesus Christ our Lord"* (Rom. 6:11).

Once again we emphasize, while we are dead to the sin nature, the sin nature itself, although dormant—at least that's the way it ought to be—is not dead.

The reason we refer to the word *sin* as the "sin nature" is because in most of the places in Romans, Chapter 6, where the word *sin* is used, in the original text, it has before that word what is referred to as the definite article. In other words, it actually says *"the* sin." This means that it's not refer-ring to particular acts of sin, but rather to the sin nature or evil nature.

Paul then said, *"Let not sin* (the sin nature) *therefore reign in your mortal body, that you should obey it in the lusts thereof"* (Rom. 6:12).

Now, if it weren't possible for the sin nature to once again reign or rule within our lives exactly as it did before conver-sion (which means that despite all of our efforts otherwise, we will then serve Satan), then Paul would not have broached the subject.

His teaching here tells us that it is quite possible for the sin nature to once again rule and reign within the heart and life of the believer, and will, in fact, do so if the believer doesn't understand his place and position in Christ.

How does this happen?

IMPROPER UNDERSTANDING OF THE CROSS

I think by now you surely know what we're going to say.

If the believer doesn't understand the Cross, and I refer to understanding the Cross as it regards our sanctification—exactly that as it regards our sanctification and exactly that which Paul taught in Romans, Chapter 6—he will then try to live for the Lord in all the wrong ways. In doing such a thing, which every believer will do if the Cross is misunderstood, in some way, failure is going to be the result.

When this happens, it's like throwing fuel on smoldering

coals of fire. Whereas the sin nature was dormant, now it flames anew, and the believer finds himself being ruled by the sin nature instead of the divine nature (II Pet. 1:4). This is a miserable state for a believer to be in, but unfortunately, it is the state of most believers simply because of their lack of understanding as it regards God's prescribed order of victory, which is the Cross of Christ.

Let the reader understand that there is only one remedy for sin, and that is the Cross of Christ. There is no other as there needs to be no other. If we take advantage of that remedy, victory will be ours, and perpetual victory at that. However, if we do not understand that prescribed order and try to live for God by means and ways other than the Cross, the end result every single time will be failure, with the sin nature ruling such a believer.

The only remedy for that situation is for the believer to understand that his victory in totality is found in what Jesus did at the Cross and his faith in that finished work. This is the manner in which the Holy Spirit works, and if our faith is properly placed, the Holy Spirit will definitely work mightily on our behalf (Rom. 8:1-2, 11).

Then, as Paul also said, *"Sin shall not have dominion over you: for you are not under the law, but under grace"* (Rom. 6:14).

FAILURE

This is the reason a failure to understand the Cross as

it refers to sanctification brings about failure in the life of believers. Please understand that the preacher is in the same category. He must have the same faith in the Cross as the layman, or he will face the same difficulty, even if God is using him.

Now, the church has tried to face this problem in many and varied ways other than the Cross. It doesn't really matter which way the church chooses, irrespective as to how good it may look on the surface. If it's not the way of the Cross, continued failure will be the result.

Let us say it again: God has only one remedy for sin, and that is the Cross of Christ. So, the church can try humanistic psychology, it can try self-efforts, it can try self-improvement, and it can try law of every description, but the end result will always be the same—failure.

WHY WON'T THE CHURCH EMBRACE THE CROSS?

Some small part of the church is embracing the Cross and is seeing tremendous results, even as the Word of God guarantees. However, the truth is, it's only a small percentage, with the far greater majority advocating other things.

Why?

The reason is either unbelief or ignorance. We'll address the latter first.

Most Christians, especially preachers, are loath to admit that they don't understand the Cross, but the truth is, most don't! The problem is pride.

Many Christians erroneously think of the Cross as something very elementary, which means that it's basic, and it's something they already know. It is as one man wrote me the other day and stated, "Why do you keep talking about the Cross? All Christians understand everything about the Cross."

The truth is, most Christians understand hardly anything about the Cross of Christ. What little understanding most Christians have about the Cross refers only to salvation, and even that is sketchy to say the least.

SANCTIFICATION

When it comes to sanctification, in other words, how we live for God and how we have victory over the world, the flesh, and the Devil, which we are addressing here, most Christians understand hardly anything at all as it regards the Cross and this all-important work within our lives. So, the results are failure on every hand, despite the believer doing everything within his power to do otherwise. In other words, any and every true Christian wants to live for God and wants to live for the Lord in the right way.

Due to the fact that the divine nature now resides within our hearts and lives, we don't want to sin. Any Christian who would claim that Christians desire to sin simply doesn't know what he is talking about. While the flesh may want something that's wrong, the spirit of the child of God definitely doesn't.

Still, that Christian will sin if he does not deny himself,

which means to deny his own ability and, thereby, take up the Cross daily in his following Christ (Lk. 9:23-24).

That's what Paul was talking about when he said, *"For the good that I would I do not: but the evil which I would not, that I do"* (Rom. 7:19).

Now, to be sure, when Paul wrote this, he full well knew God's prescribed order of victory and most definitely was walking in that victory; however, he was going back in his life after he was saved and baptized with the Holy Spirit and after he had begun to preach the gospel. Not knowing God's way, he tried to live for God as most everyone else does, by the keeping of commandments. He found to his utter dismay that this simply wouldn't work. In fact, it was to Paul that this great secret of life and living was given.

SCRIPTURAL IGNORANCE

Millions fall into the category of scriptural ignorance. If a subject is not preached and taught behind the pulpit, then it's impossible for the people to know and understand what the Word of God actually says. *"Faith comes by hearing, and hearing by the Word of God"* (Rom. 10:17).

The only way for the problem of scriptural ignorance to be solved is for the Word of God to be correctly taught as it regards the Cross.

Unbelief is another matter altogether. The longer I live for God and the more that the Lord has shown me about the Cross, the more that I believe that unbelief is the problem with many. In fact, ignorance certainly may contain a modicum of unbelief also, and probably does.

When we speak of unbelief, we're speaking of the fact that the preacher and the layman simply don't believe that the Cross of Christ is the answer for the dilemma of mankind. They may pay lip service to the Cross, but the truth is, their actions prove that their faith lies elsewhere. That's the reason the church has gone pell-mell into humanistic psychology. That's the reason its basic cry is, "You need professional help."

WHAT JESUS DID AT THE CROSS

The truth is, if we turn toward the direction of the world and worldly wisdom, this means that we have placed the Cross of Christ into default.

We either believe that Jesus Christ faced every problem at the Cross—I speak of every problem that besets humanity in the realm of sin—or else, He didn't. I happen to believe that He did.

The Scripture says: *"Blotting out the handwriting of ordinances that was against us, which was contrary to us, and took it out of the way, nailing it to His Cross. And having spoiled principalities and powers, He made a show of them openly, triumphing over them in it"* (Col. 2:14-15).

This tells us that the claims of the broken law against us were forever settled at the Cross.

There Jesus atoned for all sin. In doing so, He totally and completely defeated every demon spirit and power of darkness.

None were excluded, with all being included.

So, this means that Jesus addressed every single problem of mankind at the Cross; therefore, the Cross is the answer to man's dilemma and, in fact, the only answer.

FEAR

"And when Pharaoh drew near, the children of Israel lifted up their eyes, and, behold, the Egyptians marched after them; and they were sore afraid: and the children of Israel cried out unto the LORD" (Ex. 14:10).

Verses 10 through 12 record the complaints of Israel. The fear, unbelief, and anger of the very people who had witnessed God's wonders in the land of Egypt would appear incredible, but that each Bible student finds these evils in his own heart and learns by sad experience that great depression of mind usually follows exceptional spiritual triumphs.

Unbelief cried out, "The wilderness will become our grave," but the result was that the sea became Pharaoh's grave.

The message from the Lord is ever, *"Fear not."*

"Stand still" refers to a total lack of dependence on the flesh.

This was a sore trial of faith, and sadly, Israel did fail in the hour of testing; however, this, as well, is so often the case with us.

It doesn't matter how many times the Lord has delivered us in the past or how signally His power has been exerted on our behalf.

When some new trial comes, or even the old trial with a more fierce face, we tend to forget God's previous interventions and are swallowed up by the greatness of our present emergency, and we conduct ourselves not unlike Israel of old.

THE CHILDREN OF ISRAEL

Verse 10 says, *"The children of Israel lifted up their eyes,"* which means they observed the Egyptians coming after them. Their eyes were upon the Egyptians and not on the Lord.

How easy it is for us to look at circumstances, to look at events, and to look to the prattle of the Devil and, thereby, take our eyes off the Lord. Such always leads to disaster.

We should remember that with the exception of Joshua and Caleb, the 12 spies sent into Canaan saw only the walled cities and the giants. Joshua and Caleb saw the Lord and said: *"Only rebel not you against the LORD, neither fear you the people of the land; for they are bread for us: their defense is departed from them, and the LORD is with us: fear them not"* (Num. 14:9).

I think one can say without fear of exaggeration or contradiction that the hardest thing for the child of God to do is to keep his eyes on the Lord when circumstances are screaming very negative things. This is always the great trial of faith. As it has been well said, "Faith must always be tested, and great faith must be tested greatly."

Pharaoh had a design to ruin Israel; therefore, God had a design to ruin Pharaoh.

Henry said, "The Egyptians were angry with themselves for the best deed they ever did, which was to finally let Israel go, while the Israelites were angry with God for the greatest kindness that was ever done them, their deliverance from Egypt; thus gross are the absurdities of unbelief."

COMPLAINT

"And they said unto Moses, Because there were no graves in Egypt, have you taken us away to die in the wilderness? wherefore have you dealt thus with us, to carry us forth out of Egypt?" (Ex. 14:11).

When things do not go right, the normal reaction is for one to vent one's anger on someone else. So, the leaders in Israel would vent their anger on Moses. They were talking death when the greatest miracle the world has ever seen was about to take place. Unbelief talks this way because it looks at circumstances instead of looking to the Lord. While it is true that they cried out unto the Lord, even as the previous verse proclaims, it evidently was not a cry of faith, but rather of unbelief.

Pink said: "How absurd are the reasonings of unbelief! If death at the hands of the Egyptians was to be their lot, why had Jehovah delivered them from the land of bondage? The fact that He had led them out of Egypt was evidence enough that He was not going to allow them to fall before their enemies. Besides this, the Lord had promised that they would worship Him in Mount Horeb (Ex. 3:12). That being the case, how then could they now perish in the wilderness? But where faith is not in exercise, the promises of God bring no comfort, and afford no stay to the heart."

THE PATH CHOSEN BY GOD

While they were criticizing Moses, in reality, they were criticizing God, and in reality, that is always the case with complaining and unbelief.

Israel had been brought to their present position by God Himself. It was the pillar of cloud that had led them to where they were now encamped.

This must be an important truth for us: We must not expect the path of faith to be an easy or smooth one.

As one preacher has well said, "If it was easy, anyone could do it." But instead, as it's not easy, faith, so to speak, separates the men from the boys.

Faith must ever be tested in order that we may learn the sufficiency of God!

There are three reasons for this:

1. That we may prove from experience that He is able to supply our every need (Phil. 4:19).

2. That He can make a way of escape from every temptation, which is the way of the Cross (I Cor. 1:17; 10:13).

3. That we might be able to see that He can do for us exceedingly, abundantly above all that we ask or think (Eph. 3:20).

LET US ALONE

"Is not this the word that we did tell you in Egypt, saying, Let us alone, that we may serve the Egyptians? For it had been better for us to serve the Egyptians, than that we should die in the wilderness" (Ex. 14:12).

Why is it that it's so hard for believers to trust God?

By trusting Him, I'm speaking of the future and His care for us. There was ample proof, in fact, abundant proof, as it regarded the great miracles that God performed in the sight of all the children of Israel, affecting the entire nation of Egypt. So, there was no excuse for this unbelief and complaining, but we must ask ourselves, are we doing any better?

I will use myself and this ministry as an example.

THE WAY OF THE LORD

Since October 1991, we have had to trust God totally and completely for everything that we have. By that, I mean that if God didn't provide it, it simply could not be obtained.

Our ministry, along with Family Worship Center—our local church—is a media ministry, which reaches tremendous numbers of people, but yet, requires large sums of money. To be sure, the price per person reached is far less, and I mean greatly less, than the expenses of churches.

However, because of the great number of people reached, such demands large sums of cash. We have to pay the television stations, the cable systems, and the satellites. We had no place to get that cash except to totally and completely trust

God. Regrettably, virtually every preacher in the world was urging their people not to give to us in any capacity. So, we were cut off from sustenance and support except for the Lord. In other words, He would have to furnish a table in the wilderness, that is, if we were to survive.

Not only was our financial survival at stake, but above all, even our spiritual survival was at stake.

I can well empathize with the words of Paul when he said, *"O wretched man that I am! Who shall deliver me from the body of this death?"* (Rom. 7:24).

SEEKING THE LORD

Sadly, no one in the church, and I speak of the church world as a whole, could give me the answer to this dilemma. Of course, I'm sure there were some preachers somewhere who had the answer, but they were few and far between.

For six years I sought the Lord, and I speak of the time between October 1991 and 1997. I wept before Him day and night, asking Him to show me the way of victory for the child of God. I knew that the ways being promoted by the church simply were not scriptural. Not being scriptural, they simply would not work.

Then, in 1997, the Lord began to open up to me the Message of the Cross, emphatically stating to me, "That for which you seek is found totally and completely in the Cross, and only in the Cross."

I will never forget that hour; and to be sure, the Lord has

continued to enlarge that revelation from that day until now, and I trust the enlargement will ever continue. To be frank, the Message of the Cross of Christ is utterly inexhaustible, hence, Paul referring to it as the *"everlasting covenant"* (Heb. 13:20). It is everlasting because it is perfect. What Jesus did there cannot be improved upon simply because it doesn't need to be improved upon.

LOOK WHAT THE LORD HAS DONE ...

As mentioned, in 1997, the Lord began to open up to me the Message of the Cross. To be sure, it was not something new but actually that which had already been given to the Apostle Paul and, no doubt, others down through the march of time. However, I was to find out that the Message of the Cross, as it regards our sanctification—how we live for God and how we have victory over the world, the flesh, and the Devil—presented itself basically as an unknown factor in the modern church. In other words, for the most part, the modern church simply does not know how to live for God, even those who earnestly want to walk victoriously.

I believe it was the year 2005. At any rate, the Lord told me that I was to develop a study Bible. Actually, He had been dealing with me for several years about this but did not let me begin until the Message of the Cross became a reality. However, when the Holy Spirit said, "Now it's time," this was something I had to do. The Lord did three things:

1. He told me to develop the Expositor's Study Bible.

2. He showed me how He wanted it done.

3. He helped me to do it.

I personally believe that this is the Bible for the 21ST century. The Lord is quickly spreading this edition all over the world. Incidentally, it is King James, but it is totally unique as study Bibles go. At the present time, we have it translated it from English into Spanish, into Portuguese, and into Russian. German and French will be finished shortly.

Then, in 2010, the Lord instructed me to develop a television network that would air the gospel 24 hours a day, seven days a week. It was to be for the express purpose of preaching the Cross. He instructed me that we were not to sell time to other preachers but use the preachers here at Family Worship Center. In other words, there must not be any contradiction of the message.

Obeying the Lord, we began the network, and it was as if the Lord began to open every door in the world. At the time of this writing, approximately 1 billion people in the world can receive the Sonlife Broadcasting Network if they so desire. How we give the Lord the praise and the glory for all of this.

I personally believe that we are about to see a moving of the Holy Spirit that's going to sweep millions into the kingdom of God. I further believe that it's going to be the last great worldwide move before the coming great tribulation. To be sure, the rapture of the church is going to take place very shortly. I believe, as well, that we are going to see hundreds of thousands baptized with the Holy Spirit with the evidence of speaking with other tongues. It is the Lord's doing, and it is marvelous in His eyes. In other words, I am expecting the greatest move of God relative to souls being saved in the very near future that the world has ever witnessed or experienced. I believe the Lord has told me that this will be the case.

THE EGYPTIANS, THE WILDERNESS, AND THE DELIVERANCE

All Israel could see at this time was either slavery to the Egyptians or dying in the wilderness. Regrettably, that is the condition of many, if not most, Christians presently. They do not understand deliverance because they're looking for it in the wrong place.

As we've already explained, evil passions grip most people simply because they do not know or understand God's prescribed order of victory.

However, in the Cross, and we speak of what Jesus there did, there is deliverance for every single sinner on the face of this earth and for every single believer.

Many Christians, after trying so very, very hard, are simply at the point of giving up. They don't know what to do. They see only Egypt, allegorically speaking, or spiritual death, i.e., the wilderness. The church has said try this and try that—all to no avail.

However, exactly as the Lord had deliverance for the children of Israel, He has deliverance for every single believer presently, irrespective as to what the problem might be.

FORGIVENESS AND DELIVERANCE

Many Christians mistake forgiveness for deliverance. As wonderful and necessary as forgiveness is, forgiveness is not deliverance. What do I mean by that?

Many Christians, after failing the Lord, will ask Him to forgive them, and to be sure, He always will. He plainly tells us in His Word: *"If we confess our sins, He is faithful and just to forgive us our sins, and to cleanse us from all unrighteousness"* (I Jn. 1:9).

He meant exactly what He said and places no limitation on the number of times that He will forgive.

Whenever the believer receives forgiveness and experiences the return to peace, many times, he mistakes that for deliverance. As stated, it isn't!

With the believer being freshly forgiven and the joy and peace of the Lord instantly restored, and with him rejoicing in the feeling this brings, he sometimes mistakes this for deliverance. He then believes that the besetting sin, which has plagued him for so long, and for which he has asked and received forgiveness so many times, will now be no more, but over and over again, he has found that not to be the case.

Why?

WHAT IS DELIVERANCE?

Many Christians are loath to admit that they need deliverance. Others do admit it, but they think that a preacher can effect such by the laying on of hands, etc. Now, while laying on of hands is certainly scriptural and helpful, this is not the answer to the sin problem. Were it the answer, Jesus would not have had to come down here and die on a Cross. That should be understood. Others have been beset by a problem so long that they have come to believe that they are demon possessed. They then seek for a preacher who will either cast out the so-called demon or effect their deliverance, once again, by the laying on of hands. That doesn't work either.

In the first place, while demon spirits definitely are involved in all manner of sin, especially bondages of sin, no Christian can be demon possessed. He can be oppressed but not possessed! There is a reason that demon spirits, which cause untold problems and troubles, have the latitude they have as it regards many Christians

FAITH PLACED IN THE WRONG THING

The problem with such Christians is not these things we have mentioned, plus many we haven't mentioned, but rather their faith is placed in wrong things.

Now, let's say that again: To properly walk in victory before the Lord and the world, in other words to have and maintain victory over the world, the flesh, and the Devil, the object of our faith must ever be the Cross of Christ. This is supremely important. If our faith is in something else, even as we've already said several times, in the eyes of the Lord, we are actually committing spiritual adultery.

Understanding that, we should surely know that the Holy Spirit, whom we must have working within our hearts and lives mightily, that is, if we are to walk in victory, simply will not function in that type of atmosphere, as should be obvious (Rom. 7:1-4). While He certainly will remain with us, He will not exhibit His power under such circumstances.

WALKING AFTER THE FLESH

"There is therefore now no condemnation to them which are in Christ Jesus, who walk not after the flesh, but after the Spirit" (Rom. 8:1).

From this passage, we know and realize that it's possible for a Christian to *"walk after the flesh."*

Exactly what is walking after the flesh?

It is the placing of our faith in anything, irrespective as to what it is, other than the Cross of Christ.

The *flesh*, as Paul used the word, is that which is indicative of a human being. It's our personal strength, education, motivation, talent, ability, etc., in other words, what a human being can do.

We must understand that what we as believers are facing in the spiritual world, and I speak of fallen angels and demon spirits, cannot be overcome by our ability, no matter how great it might be. It can only be overcome by the Holy Spirit. If we are looking to ourselves in any manner instead of Christ and the Cross, this stops the Holy Spirit from helping us because we are then walking after the flesh.

Now, let's look at walking after the Spirit. What does that mean?

It doesn't refer to doing spiritual things, as important as that might be. It simply refers to our faith being placed exclusively in Christ and the Cross. When we speak of the Cross, of course, we aren't speaking of the wooden beam on which Jesus died, but rather what He there accomplished.

Walking after the Spirit (Rom. 8:1-11) means that the believer has ceased to walk after the flesh, which means he has placed his faith exclusively in the Cross of Christ. The moment he begins to walk after the Spirit, he will find that deliverance now is his. With some people, the deliverance will come instantly. With others, it will not. With some, Satan will come against them harder than they have ever experienced him previously. It will be confusing because they think that all of a sudden victory is going to be theirs, and they find it's not.

However, if the believer will persist, will hold on, and will not move his faith elsewhere, there will come an hour, whatever that time frame might be, that sin will no longer have dominion over us (Rom. 6:14).

That doesn't mean sinless perfection, but it does mean that we are not to be dominated by sin in any fashion.

So many of us have learned so many things that are unscriptural and are wrong, and the Holy Spirit has to divest us of them. That takes time! To be sure, it takes no time for the Lord, but it takes time for us. In other words, He has to empty us before He can fill us.

This is God's prescribed order of victory, and His only prescribed order. Let us say it again: it is the Cross of Christ.

FEAR NOT

"And Moses said unto the people, Fear you not, stand still, and see the salvation of the LORD, which He will show to you today: for the Egyptians whom you have seen today, you shall see them again no more forever" (Ex. 14:13).

Several wonderful things are said in this passage, so wonderful, in fact, that they defy all description. In this verse, we have a compendium of our present spiritual experience as well. We would do well to heed what is being said here because it applies to us figuratively just as it applied to Israel literally.

From the phrase, *"And Moses said unto the people,"* we learn what the preacher is supposed to preach. In essence, Moses, in shadow and type, preached the Cross (I Cor. 1:23). What Moses told the people is what we as preachers of the gospel are to tell the people as well. If we veer or err from this message, whatever it is we tell the people will not bring victory to their lives, but rather the very opposite. Tragically, there are precious few preachers today truly preaching the Cross. However, let the preacher know and understand that preaching the Cross is the only message that will set the captive free and then keep the person free. That's why Paul said, *"For I determined not to know anything among you, save Jesus Christ, and Him crucified"* (I Cor. 2:2).

For those preachers who would preach other things as an answer to man's dilemma, they are blatantly, openly, and purposely ignoring the plain Word given here by the Holy Spirit to Paul.

THE CROSS OF CHRIST

If it is to be noticed, in I Corinthians 2:2, Paul didn't substitute the word *resurrection* for the word *crucified*.

While he certainly preached a resurrected Christ as we, as well, are to do, it was not the resurrection, as important and as necessary as that was, that delivered humanity from the powers of darkness, but rather the Cross of Christ (Gal. 1:4).

Moses told Israel to *"fear not."* If the message is right, which means that the faith of the individual hearing the message is now right, the believer has no cause to fear.

There was a great difference in the children of Israel during their day than our position presently.

They were depending on a miracle that had not yet been brought about, while we are looking to a miracle that has already been brought about, and I speak of what Christ did for us at the Cross.

If Moses would tell the children of Israel to fear not even though the miracle had not yet been brought to pass, how much more are we being told by the Holy Spirit presently to fear not!

They were asked to trust in a work that had not yet been

completed, while we now are told to trust in a work that has been gloriously and wondrously completed.

FEAR NOT

The point is, if they had no occasion to fear, how much more presently do we have no occasion to fear?

Fear what? They were fearing that the Egyptians would overtake them and slaughter them where they stood.

Now, read carefully what I have to say: If you as a believer are not trusting in Christ and His Cross, in other words, if the Cross of Christ is not the object of your faith, I can assure you that you have every reason to fear.

In fact, I have no doubt that some of you holding this book in your hands greet each morning with fear. You wonder if you will make it through another day. You are fighting and struggling, but yet, you are losing. You fear that you will be found out, and above all, you fear that you might even lose your soul.

Regrettably, the majority of the modern church falls into this latter category. They live a life of fear, and I speak of those who truly love God, and it's because they are trusting in something that's not biblical. What do I mean by that?

IT IS NOT BIBLICAL

To make it simple and easy to understand, it means that the believer has placed his faith in something other than

Christ and Him crucified, and it really doesn't matter what the other thing might be or even how holy it might be in its own right.

The Cross of Christ and faith in that finished work are the only means of salvation and victory that God has afforded. He has nothing else because He needs nothing else.

If you place your faith in that finished work, and maintain it in that finished work, you need never fear, and to be sure, you won't fear because you're standing on the rock.

The storms may come and they may go, but you will be unmoved.

THAT'S WHY THE PSALMIST SAID...

"Blessed is the man who walks not in the counsel of the ungodly, nor stands in the way of sinners, nor sits in the seat of the scornful. But His delight is in the law of the LORD; and in His law does he meditate day and night. And He shall be like a tree planted by the rivers of water, that brings forth His fruit in His season; His leaf also shall not wither; and whatsoever He does shall prosper" (Ps. 1:1-3).

To be frank, this man of whom the psalmist speaks is Christ. Inasmuch as we are *"in Christ,"* then it applies to us, as well, but only as we are "in Christ." To be sure, we are in Christ by virtue of our faith in Him and what He has done for us regarding His finished work.

Paul said, *"But God forbid that I should glory, save in the Cross of our Lord Jesus Christ, by whom the world is crucified unto me, and I unto the world"* (Gal. 6:14).

STAND STILL

This would seem to be the simplest thing to do, but yet, it is actually the hardest thing to do. All attempts at self-help must end. All activities of the flesh must cease. The workings of nature must be subdued. This is the right attitude and, in fact, the only attitude of faith in the presence of a trial—stand still.

Now, this is impossible to flesh and blood. All who know in any measure the restlessness of the human heart under anticipated trial and difficulty will be able to form some concept of what is involved in standing still. By contrast, nature must be doing something. It will rush hither and thither. Somehow, in all the activity, it thinks there is safety when, in reality, the very opposite is true.

Unbelief creates or magnifies difficulties and then sets us about removing them, or rather attempting to remove them, by our own bustling and fruitless actions, which, in reality, do not remove anything.

The flesh must always do something, while faith, by contrast, trusts in something that has already been done.

Let us ask this question: Do you think you can deliver yourself from the powers of darkness by your own strength and ability? Can the sinner save his own soul? Can the Christian formulate his own victory, which means to subdue the powers of darkness?

Concerning this, the Prophet Jeremiah said, *"Can the Ethiopian change his skin, or the leopard his spots? then may you also do good, who are accustomed to do evil"* (Jer. 13:23).

SO, WHAT DOES IT MEAN TO ACTUALLY STAND STILL?

This is what Jesus was speaking about when He said, *"If any man will come after Me, let him deny himself, and take up his cross daily, and follow Me"* (Lk. 9:23).

When He spoke of one denying oneself, He wasn't speaking of asceticism (a denial of all things that may give pleasure) as many think, but rather the denying of our own strength and ability. We are rather to look to the Cross, which refers to what Jesus there did, and actually do so on a daily basis.

So, standing still simply means that we do not trust our own strength and ability, but rather Christ, and more particularly, what He did at the Cross on our behalf. In other words, we're trusting in a work that's already been done.

When we try to bring something about by our activity, whatever it might be, we are, in effect, saying that what Christ did at the Cross was insufficient and that we have to do something else. What does the Scripture say about Christ?

PAUL

Paul wrote, *"Who* (Christ) *being the brightness of His*

glory (the glory of the Father), *and the express image of His person* (the express image of the Father), *and upholding all things by the word of His power, when He had by Himself purged our sins* (which He did at the Cross), *sat down on the right hand of the majesty on high"* (Heb. 1:3).

Jesus *"sat down on the right hand of the majesty on high"* simply because what He did at the Cross, as Paul stated, finished the task; hence, it is referred to as a finished work. In fact, Paul also referred to the new covenant as an everlasting covenant, simply meaning that there will never be a need for another covenant (Heb. 13:20).

So, standing still refers to total trust in a work that has already been completed, meaning that we do not have to do anything else.

THE SALVATION OF THE LORD

"And see the salvation of the LORD." Please notice that it is the salvation of the LORD, which refers to the victory of the Lord and means that it is totally and completely of Him and not at all of us. Thus it is with salvation and, in fact, every single thing that we receive from the Lord. None of it is from us or of us, but rather from Him and by virtue of His sacrificial atoning work at the Cross.

In fact, that's why we are to stand still. It is simply because none of this is of us, and all of it is of Him, and is all made possible by what He did on the Cross. So, when we involve ourselves in some type of spiritual activity, thinking that such will bring about victory, we find the very opposite to be the case. It is only faith that will bring about victory, and more specifically, faith in Christ and Him crucified.

Hence, Paul said, *"For we through the Spirit wait for the hope of righteousness by faith"* (Gal. 5:5).

WHICH HE WILL SHOW YOU TODAY

As the Lord was going to deliver Israel that very day, likewise, for the modern believers who place their faith totally and completely in Christ and the Cross, victory will come that very day. There may or may not be a struggle in the flesh, but victory is theirs the moment that faith is properly placed. As well, the struggle may continue for a period of time. In fact, it could continue even for several years in one way or the other; however, the believer will sense in his spirit that he is gaining strength every day, and to be sure, the realization of victory will ultimately come in totality.

The Scripture clearly and plainly states: *"For sin shall not have dominion over you: for you are not under the law, but under grace"* (Rom. 6:14).

YOU WILL SEE THEM NO MORE FOREVER

"For the Egyptians whom you have seen today, you shall see them again no more forever": A better translation would be: "For as you have seen the Egyptians today, you shall see them again no more forever."

In other words, they had seen the Egyptians in a menacing, destructive manner, intent upon totally destroying the children of Israel, which it looked like they would certainly do. It didn't mean that they would never again see any Egyptians, but it meant that they would never see them in this posture of what looked like victory for the Egyptians.

It is the same with the modern believer who places his faith exclusively in Christ and His great sacrifice. While Satan has sought to destroy you in the past, and at times, it looked like he would succeed, you will see him no more in this posture. You will see him as a defeated foe because you understand how he was defeated.

HOW WAS SATAN DEFEATED?

He was defeated exclusively by what Christ did at the Cross. Jesus never grappled or physically wrestled with Satan. To be frank, Satan doesn't want any part of Christ in any capacity.

When Jesus died on the Cross, through His death, which necessitated the shedding of His blood, He satisfied the terrible sin debt that was against us.

The Scripture said that He nailed the requirements of the law *"to His Cross."*

When He did this, this took away Satan's legal right to hold man in captivity because of man's sin.

In other words, sin is the legal right that Satan has to place man in captivity.

However, with all sin atoned, which Jesus did at the Cross, this completely *"spoiled principalities and powers,"* making *"a show of them openly, triumphing over them in it"* (Col. 2:14-15).

As the believer understands that, to be sure, he will never again see Satan in a posture of victory. In other words, Satan's victory over him in any capacity has now come to an end. Satan steals, kills, and destroys (Jn. 10:10). In that capacity, with his faith properly placed, which refers to being placed entirely in the Cross, the believer will see him no more, at least in that capacity.

In that regard, it is forever. Hallelujah!

THE LORD SHALL FIGHT FOR YOU

"The LORD shall fight for you, and you shall hold your peace" (Ex. 14:14).

The Lord could fight for Israel only as long as they stood still. Had they turned and tried to fight the Egyptians themselves in any capacity, this would have hindered the Lord fighting for them, and they, no doubt, would have been defeated.

Someone has well said, "In justification, the Lord fights for us, and in sanctification, He fights in us."

Verse 14 is very dear to me personally, and in two ways especially.

The first way involves a very trying time in my life and ministry.

I want to relate to you how the Lord used this very verse to bring victory.

THE LORD WILL DEFEND YOU

While there are certainly some godly preachers and laity in Pentecostal denominations, still, if I understand the Word of God correctly, it is my belief that the majority of these denominations are functioning under law instead of grace. As well, their government has long since, at least for most of them, ceased to be scriptural.

If, in fact, that is true, preachers would do well to get out of these denominations, and, as well, the laity would do well to find other churches. As it regards the laity, there certainly may be the case where some churches in these respective denominations are led by godly pastors. If that is the case, they certainly should remain where they are but with the understanding that the problems that I have mentioned, as it regards these denominations, could invade their own partic-ular churches at any time.

Concerning my own personal situation, one particular denomination set out to completely destroy any ministry that I might have. They used any method at their disposal, with nothing to be excluded. To be frank, I actually feared for my life.

This would be wrong if a preacher were a member of such a denomination, but considering that he's no longer a member of such a group, it becomes even worse.

It's one thing to withdraw fellowship, but it's something else altogether to deny the blood of Christ, which they did, and then to take it into their own hands to wreck any ministry that one might have left.

THE CHURCH IN THESE LAST DAYS

Jesus said, *"The kingdom of heaven is like unto leaven, which a woman took, and hid in three measures of meal, till the whole was leavened"* (Mat. 13:33).

In effect, Christ was referring to the church as a whole and how it would be in the last days.

When a woman is used in this fashion in Scripture, it is always in an evil sense. The meal is a symbol of the Word of God. The leaven is, of course, a type of sin.

The idea is, the church in the last days, at least as a whole, will be completely leavened, which means that the Word of God will be so corrupted that it will no longer be of any use.

Sadly and regrettably, this of which Jesus said is the condition of the modern church. In fact, the church presently has never been in such a negative spiritual condition as it is presently, at least since the Reformation. It falls into the category of the Laodicean Church, which Jesus addressed.

He said: *"Because you say, I am rich, and increased with goods, and have need of nothing; and know not that you are wretched, and miserable, and poor, and blind, and naked: I counsel you to buy of Me gold tried in the fire, that you may be rich; and white raiment, that you may be clothed, and that the shame of your nakedness do not appear; and anoint your eyes with eyesalve, that you may see"* (Rev. 3:17-18).

The wounds of the enemy hurt; however, the wounds of those who are your own hurt far more.

A PERSONAL EXPERIENCE

The year was 1988, and the month was May, if I remember correctly. Information came to us regarding certain things this denomination had done and were then beginning to do. These things, which I will leave nameless, were so insidious, so evil, and so wicked that they defied description. As stated, I feared for my life.

On the particular afternoon that this information came to us, I will confess, I did not sleep at all that night. For some part of the night, I walked up and down on our driveway in front of our house, seeking the Lord, asking Him as to what I should do.

At that particular time, I really did not receive any answer from the Lord.

A little after daylight, I made up my mind that I would take steps to defend myself. When our office opened, I called our television department and told them to prepare a special that we would tape that afternoon. I planned to lay everything out as to exactly what this denomination was doing and to air it over our telecast, which covered almost all of this nation and even other countries of the world.

For one to defend oneself, I suppose, is a basic instinct; however, when we do such, we are, in effect, taking ourselves out from under the hand of the Lord, thereby, hindering His defense on our behalf. Now, there are certainly times when an answer should be given, but as I was to find out, the way I was going about this was wrong.

While I was waiting for everything to be prepared, our two grandsons, Gabriel and Matthew, came over to the house. If I remember correctly, Gabriel was 6 years old at that time, and Matthew was 5. They wanted to go swimming in our pool, and I walked outside with them to watch them while they played in the water, etc.

To be sure, my heart was very, very heavy. It seemed as if the weight of the world was on my shoulders, and I had nowhere to turn as it regarded others—outside of my family and our church, Family Worship Center.

THE ANSWER TO PRAYER

I can still visualize this scene in my mind as to what happened, which was such a blessing to me.

Even though I had given instructions for the television program to be made, which I would do shortly, in my spirit, I didn't feel right about the situation. Then it happened: The Lord would now answer my prayer, for which I had cried to Him most of the night.

Frances came out the door holding the Bible in her hands. If I remember, she was weeping. She said to me the following:

"I was reading Chapter 14 of Exodus, and when I came to Verse 14, '*The* LORD *shall fight for you, and you shall hold your peace,*' the presence of the Lord came all over me." Then she said, "Is the Lord telling us something in this?"

I took her Bible and looked at the Scripture, and when I did, the Spirit of God came on me as well. I, too, began to weep, for I knew that this was the Lord's answer to my dilemma.

After praising the Lord for a period of time and feeling great peace within my soul, I called our office and told them to stop all preparation as it regarded the television program that I had planned to make. Frances and I agreed at that moment that we would put all of this in the hands of the Lord and would not try to defend ourselves, in effect, holding our peace and letting the Lord fight for us.

I will confess that this was hard to do at times because the onslaught didn't let up when we made this decision. However, I had the promise of God, and that's all that mattered.

WHAT HAPPENED?

As I dictate these notes, I've never been stronger in the Lord, for which I give Him all the praise and all the glory. As well, the ministry is exploding all over the world. At the time of this writing, our network, which operates 24 hours a day, seven days a week, goes into some 72 million homes in America and well over 100 million in other countries of the world. In fact, nearly 3 billion people can receive the programming if they so desire. That's how God has abundantly blessed. The letters we are receiving concerning people being saved and lives being changed are miraculous to say the least.

Had I tried to defend myself, thereby, ignoring what the Lord told us, I do not personally think this ministry would even be in existence today, and if it were, it would be on a much smaller scale.

In fact, had I not sought His face earnestly, asking Him for leading and guidance, I'm not so sure that guidance would have been given. If, in fact, that had been the case, I don't think we would have survived. The Lord did fight for us, and He did so grandly and gloriously, and we give Him all the praise and all the glory.

SPIRITUAL VICTORY

Now, I want to deal with the second way that this passage is so dear to me and, in reality, should be dear to every single believer.

At this juncture, when Israel was about to cross the Red Sea, where God would perform one of His greatest miracles, what the Lord was to do for them was that which would happen very shortly. In other words, even though it would shortly come to pass, it had not then happened. However, it most definitely would, and it most definitely did.

The fight of which I now speak has already been accomplished, and I refer to what Jesus did at the Cross. There He overcame every single power of darkness, excluding nothing of Satan and including Satan himself.

Until 1997, while I understood the Cross as it regarded salvation, and I preached it strongly and saw the world touched by the power of the gospel, the facts were, I did not understand the Cross as it regarded sanctification. To be factual, there aren't but a handful of Christians in the world presently, that is, when we consider the whole, who understand the Cross as it refers to sanctification, in other words, how we live for God on a daily basis. To not understand it in this fashion guarantees a life of spiritual defeat.

THE MESSAGE OF THE CROSS

And yet, Paul dealt more with this subject than he did anything else. In fact, the entirety of his 14 epistles is either taken up totally with this teaching, or else, alludes to it strongly. That being the case, why is it that most Christians, and even most preachers, little understand that of which the great apostle taught?

I think Satan fights the Message of the Cross as he fights nothing else. If he can keep the gospel of the Cross of Christ from being preached as it regards salvation, he can stop sinners from being saved. Regrettably, he has succeeded tremendously so in most churches. As well, if he can stop the preacher from understanding and teaching the Cross as it regards sanctification, he can rob the Christian of victory, and he has succeeded tremendously so in this capacity also.

When we read Chapter 7 of Romans, we are reading

Paul's personal experience of trying to live for God after he was saved and baptized with the Holy Spirit, but yet, not knowing and understanding the Message of the Cross, the understanding of which the Lord would later give to him. He failed miserably, and if Paul failed miserably, where do you think that leaves us?

At any rate, if fighting the Devil will bring one victory, then, to be sure, I would have had victory as no other human being. I put up one great fight, but as all who engage in such a conflict, I was the loser, as all are the losers in that capacity.

A FAILURE TO UNDERSTAND THE WORD

This is a fight in which we must not engage simply because Jesus has already defeated Satan, even as we've already addressed.

Our major problem is that we simply do not properly understand the Word of God in many capacities. We think we do, but the truth is, we don't. To not understand the Word is to not understand the instructions, which, as should be obvious, leaves us in a predicament.

We misinterpret the Word, and I think I know the reason.

The foundation of all that God does for us and with us is the Cross of Christ. That means the foundation of the Word of God is the Cross. Actually, an understanding of the Cross was given, which, in effect, was the Word of God, even before the Word came to the world in written form. We find it in Chapter 4 of Genesis.

Evidently, immediately after the fall, the Lord had told the first family how they were to have communion with Him and experience forgiveness of sin, etc. It would be by the slain lamb, an innocent victim, which would be a type of the coming Redeemer, namely Christ.

Of course, that instruction was the Word of the Lord, but it is noteworthy to understand that the very first Word given pertained to the Cross.

So, I think the main reason people misinterpret the Word of God is simply because their faith is not anchored in the Cross, but rather in other things. If our faith is anchored in other things, no matter how good those things might be in their own right, this means that we are depending on self in some way. It's for certain that we will go wrong because outside of Christ and Him crucified, our knowledge of God is very skewed.

To say it another way, if we have a proper knowledge of Christ and the Cross, we will have a proper knowledge of the Word of God. Otherwise, our interpretation will be skewed in some manner.

SALVATION

At the moment the believing sinner comes to Christ, he is free from sin and every bondage. If at that moment he is taught the Message of the Cross, and taught it correctly, he will then understand the Word of God and avoid many pitfalls that could not be avoided otherwise.

As I have said elsewhere in this volume, in October 1991, I laid my Bible on the table in front of me. I made the statement to the people sitting there that day: "I don't know the answer, but I know that the answer to living a victorious, overcoming, Christian life is found in this book, and by the grace of God, I'm going to find that answer."

Almost immediately, the Lord gave me instructions to begin prayer meetings, which we did. Those prayer meetings continue unto this hour, at least as it regards my personal involvement. Over and over again, the Lord would speak to my heart while in prayer and would give me strength and encouragement.

However, it was not until 1997, in fact, when I began to study the book of Romans as it regarded writing that particular commentary, that the Holy Spirit began to open up to me what Paul was actually saying.

Even though I don't remember the exact date or the day, I definitely do remember what took place in my soul. At the moment that the Holy Spirit began to reveal to me the truth, I knew it was the answer for which I had so long sought.

In fact, a few days later, in one of the morning prayer meetings, the Spirit of the Lord clearly said to my heart the following in three parts:

1. "The answer for which you seek is found in the Cross."
2. "The solution for which you seek is found in the Cross."
3. "The answer for which you seek is found *only* in the Cross."

I will never forget that moment! I sat there on the floor for a period of time, weeping, as I realized the great truth, as simple as it was, that was being revealed to me.

THE HOLY SPIRIT

A few days later while teaching over our daily 90-minute morning radio program, *A Study In The Word*, the Spirit of God opened it up a little further and told me the manner and the way in which He works within our hearts and lives.

He told me that He functions entirely within the parameters of the Cross of Christ, in other words, the Cross gives Him the legal right, one might say, to function as He does.

He then took me to Romans 8:2: *"For the law of the Spirit of life in Christ Jesus has made me free from the law of sin and death,"* which portrayed to me from the Scripture exactly what He had spoken to my heart.

It is all *"in Christ Jesus,"* which always and without exception refers to Christ and what He did for us at the Cross.

I then learned who I was in Christ and the victory that He afforded me, and every believer for that matter, by His sacrificial, atoning work.

AN OVERCOMER

Millions of Christians read the statements given by Christ in Revelation, Chapters 2 and 3, about being an overcomer and immediately realize the great significance of these statements and, thereby, set out to be an overcomer. That is a position to which you will never attain by that manner. The truth is, every single believer in the world is already an overcomer.

We are that not according to the things we have done or not done, but because of what Christ did at the Cross and our constant faith in that work. That is so with every believer. So, how do I function accordingly?

I am what He has done for me by faith in His sacrificial work. Always and without exception, it's by faith (Eph. 2:8-9; Gal. 5:5-6).

At this moment, millions of Christians are trying to do things, thinking that the doing of these things, whatever they might be, will make them overcomers. Regrettably, the only thing that it will do is develop self-righteousness, which is, one might say, a stage of spiritual cancer.

It really doesn't matter what one might do—I speak of engaging in spiritual activity, whatever it might be—one simply cannot work oneself into the position of overcomer.

CRUCIFIED WITH CHRIST

Listen to what Paul said: *"I am crucified with Christ* (this takes us back to Romans 6:3-5): *nevertheless I live; yet not I, but Christ lives in me: and the life which I now live in the flesh* (our daily walk before God) *I live by the faith of the Son of God* ('the faith' being Christ and His finished work), *who loved me, and gave Himself for me"* (Gal. 2:20).

If the believer attempts to live for Christ in any other manner, the believer is going to find himself in deep trouble.

Notice what the apostle said. He didn't say, *"I am resurrected with Christ,"* even though that definitely is and was true and is definitely very important. He rather said, as the Holy Spirit guided him, *"I am crucified with Christ."*

Let the reader understand that your salvation hasn't come to you, and neither has your victory come to you, by the resurrection of Christ, as important as that is, but rather by the crucifixion of Christ.

The Word of Faith people claim that if one preaches the Cross, one is preaching death. In other words, they are telling the people to forsake the Cross or ignore the Cross, with them even repudiating the Cross. So, you can accept that erroneous, fallacious doctrine, or you can accept what Paul said, *"I am crucified with Christ."* You can't have it both ways.

It's either Paul, or else it's the leaven of the Word of Faith heresy, and heresy it is!

The day that I learned that the Lord has already fought for me, and did so at the Cross, and that my life and victory are in what He did and not what I have done, that was the day that I learned to live (Col. 2:10-15).

GO FORWARD

"And the LORD said unto Moses, Wherefore do you cry unto Me? speak unto the children of Israel, that they go

forward" (Ex. 14:15).

The time had now come. Everything previous to this was, in essence, a dress rehearsal, one might say.

The children of Israel were crying unto the Lord, but their cry was not of faith, but rather of defeat. They complained and accused Moses, which was the same as accusing God. Let us address ourselves to such a situation.

As should be understood, the Lord hears every single thing that we say. So, what are we saying?

Are we mouthing words of defeat, complaint, indecision, unbelief, etc.? Every time we do this, and to be sure, all of us have, we are insulting God.

We are, in effect, saying that He cannot handle the situation, cannot see us through, and cannot give us victory despite all that He has done in the past.

Every time we open our mouths, that which comes out should be words of faith, trust, confidence, and power. The Lord is grossly displeased with our unbelief, and that's exactly what our complaining amounts to.

At the same time, He is greatly pleased with our words of faith and confidence, irrespective of what the circumstances might be.

Whenever we praise the Lord, and do so in any fashion, we are, in effect, saying, "God can!" We are saying the same thing that God said to Israel of old, *"Go forward."*

There is no retreat as it regards the life and the living of the child of God. If we go backward, the Old Testament term of "backsliding" comes into play.

It's always, *"Go forward!"* It doesn't matter what the situation might be, what the circumstances are, or how things look, the word is still, *"Go forward!"* If we don't go forward, we will quickly find ourselves residing in a place that God has already left.

DIFFICULTIES

As is obvious here, going forward was not exactly a simple task. The Red Sea lay in front of them, so how could they go forward?

This tells us that while obstacles and difficulties may be such to us, they aren't such to God. They matter little to Him. He has said, *"Go forward,"* and that doesn't mean that we are to do so providing the way is clear. In fact, faith always goes forward, and it doesn't really matter, as stated, what the obstacles might be. The Lord has already formed a plan to take care of those obstacles, whatever they might be. Faith has no reverse, and unbelief has no forward.

Some have stated that if they hear the command, *"Go forward,"* that's what they will do; however, their thinking is wrong.

In the first place, the command to go forward has already been given. The Word of God is full of that of which we speak. In fact, the very foundation of all that we are in Christ, which is by faith, screams, *"Go forward!"* As stated, that's what faith is. So, quit waiting for something that, in fact, has already come.

DIVIDE THE SEA

"But you lift up your rod, and stretch out your hand over the sea, and divide it: and the children of Israel shall go on dry ground through the midst of the sea" (Ex. 14:16).

With the command to go forward came the provision of grace. Now would begin one of the greatest miracles ever performed.

Hebrews 11:29 says, *"By faith they passed through the Red Sea as by dry land."* From this, it is very clear that the waters of the Red Sea did not begin to divide until the feet of the Israelites came to the very brink, otherwise, they would have crossed by sight and not by faith.

As well, it seems that the sea did not open completely at once, but only the part that was next to those in the lead of the children of Israel.

As someone has said, "It does not require faith to begin a journey when I can see all the way through: but to begin when I can merely see the first step, this is faith."

Unbelievers claim that this portion of the Red Sea was only a few inches deep. Of course, that is foolishness; however, the Scripture says that they walked across on dry ground.

Again, the entirety of the army of Egypt drowned in these waters as the sea closed on them. I hardly think that an entire army of Egyptians would have drowned in just a few inches of water.

It seems that men are desperate to disprove God.
Why?

Unbelief has an evil heart, and that's about the only reason that can be given.

HONOR

"And I, behold, I will harden the hearts of the Egyptians, and they shall follow them: and I will get Me honor upon Pharaoh, and upon all his host, upon his chariots, and upon his horsemen. And the Egyptians shall know that I am the LORD, *when I have gotten Me honor upon Pharaoh, upon his chariots, and upon his horsemen"* (Ex. 14:17-18).

We should realize from these two verses that the honor of the Lord was at stake as it regarded His people and His dealing with the Egyptians. The idea is, He could deliver them, or He couldn't deliver them. Therefore, by their stubbornness, the Egyptians had placed themselves in a position to where the Lord was left with no choice but to bring destruction upon them. His honor was impugned. All of us should take a lesson from this.

On the part of the Egyptians, especially after the Lord had revealed Himself in performing miracle after miracle, they would obey as it regarded letting Israel go, or else, they would suffer the consequences. As stated, the honor of the Lord was at stake.

As it regarded the children of Israel, it didn't matter what it took to deliver them or how difficult the miracle might be; the honor of the Lord was at stake, and to be sure, the miracle would be performed, irrespective of its degree.

In fact, it would seem that the Lord made the situation about as hard as it could be made in order that He might be honored.

As it regards each believer, the honor of the Lord is always at stake, and there is only one thing that will satisfy His honor, and that is the believer evidencing faith in the Word of God.

Each believer must understand that he is a part of the greatest thing in sight of heaven. It is a way, or rather a plan, that was formulated even before the foundation of the world (I Pet. 1:18-20).

In this great plan of God, as stated, the honor of the Lord is at stake. The only way that honor can be properly satisfied is for the believer to ever evidence faith in Christ and what Christ has done at the Cross.

THE PILLAR OF THE CLOUD

"And the angel of God, which went before the camp of Israel, removed and went behind them; and the pillar of the cloud went from before their face, and stood behind them: And it came between the camp of the Egyptians and the camp of Israel: and it was a cloud and darkness to them, but it gave light by night to these: so that the one came not near the other all the night" (Ex. 14:19-20).

The angel of God spoken of in Verse 19 is actually a preincarnate appearance of the Lord Jesus Christ. The Lord Jesus is Jehovah, and one might say, the Jehovah of the Old Testament. He placed Himself between Israel and the enemy—this was protection indeed. Before Egypt could touch one single Israelite, they would have to come through the Almighty, and I think we all know how impossible that would be. Thus it is that God ever places Himself between His people and every enemy so that no weapon formed against us can prosper (Isa. 54:17).

Even above our protection, through what He did at the Cross, He has placed Himself between us and our sins. What a privilege! What a wonder! What glory!

LIGHT BY NIGHT

Concerning this, Mackintosh said: "In the same manner, the believer may look for his difficulties, and not find them, because God is between him and them."

There was a double aspect to this pillar of the cloud that stood between the Egyptians and the Israelites. While it *"gave light by night"* to the children of Israel, it was *"a cloud and darkness"* to the Egyptians.

Concerning this, Mackintosh also said: "How like the Cross of our Lord Jesus Christ! Truly, that Cross has a double aspect likewise. It forms the foundation of the believer's peace, and at the same time seals the condemnation of a guilty world. The self-same blood which purges the believer's conscience, and gives him perfect peace, stains this earth, and consummates its guilt. The very mission of the Son of God, which strips the world of its cloak, and leaves it wholly without excuse, clothes the church with a fair mantle of righteousness, and fills her mouth with ceaseless praise."

He then said: "The very same Lamb who will terrify, by His unmitigated wrath, all tribes and classes of earth, will lead by His gentle hand, His blood-bought flock through the green pastures and beside the still waters forever!" (Rev. 6:15-17; 7:13-17).

THE MIRACLE

"And Moses stretched out his hand over the sea; and the LORD *caused the sea to go back by a strong east wind all that night, and made the sea dry land, and the waters were divided"* (Ex. 14:21).

The strong east wind that God used to push a path through the sea was a divine miracle, not something accomplished by the mere forces of nature itself.

Not only was this done suddenly by a divine power, but it was likewise undone suddenly by the same power.

A wind blowing strong enough to make a path through the sea, which was approximately 12 miles across, and hold the waters up like a wall some 75 to 100 feet high, would have been strong enough to blow all the Israelites and Egyptians away, as well, had God not directed it.

Hebrews, Chapter 11, suggests that Israel had to keep believing while passing through the Red Sea so that the waters would not overwhelm them. The Egyptians did not have to exercise any faith at all, for they saw the open road before them, yet they were drowned. The way of faith is life to the redeemed but death to the rebellious.

The indication is that the children of Israel began to walk out into the sea, with God opening it before them. In other words, it seems that the entirety of the sea was not opened all at one time but, as stated, did so at about the pace that a person could slowly walk.

As to exactly how wide this path through the Red Sea was, we aren't told. However, it may have been at least a mile wide, which would have enabled the greater part of the entirety of the body of the children of Israel to walk across at the same time, with at least the ones in the rear not being too very far back from those in the lead.

THE PRESENCE OF GOD

It seems that the pillar of cloud brought up the rear-guard, which would have posed itself between the children of Israel and the Egyptians. This was the presence of God. The presence of the Lord, which had been leading them, now removed and went behind them. In effect, this meant that while they had been led by the presence of God heretofore, that presence was no longer leading them but was standing guard at the rear.

We should take a lesson from this. Sometimes the Lord withdraws Himself in grief or even in anger, but more often, He does so in mercy. This is something that He desires to teach us.

More than likely, the children of Israel little understood why the Lord had shifted from the front to the back. Whether it caused them consternation or not, we aren't told. They just knew that Moses had stated, *"Go forward."* Therefore, they would obey, which the Lord requires of us.

However, even though the presence of the Lord had shifted His position, He was doing so for the benefit of His people. They were in more danger from the Egyptians than they were from the water.

God can control the elements, and He can control man; nevertheless, the control of man is a different aspect altogether.

The elements do not have a will of their own, while man definitely does.

So, the Lord would position Himself between the children of Israel and their greatest danger, the Egyptians.

GEOGRAPHY

The area where the children of Israel are believed to have crossed is now dry land, made that way through the many centuries of gradual change, which happens all over the world for that matter. It has passed into permanent dry land.

The location was probably in the vicinity of the modern Suez Canal between the Bitter Lakes. These lakes were then a part of the gulf.

The width is anyone's guess, estimated to be anywhere from one mile across to as much as 12 to 15 miles.

Considering the location, it was probably closer to 10 to 12 miles wide. Its depth was probably—and it's only a guess—at anywhere between 20 and 40 feet.

The strong east wind that the Lord caused had to be directed by Jehovah, or else, it would have blown away the children of Israel as well as the Egyptians. In fact, it was directed at a particular part of the sea and held to that particular point.

DRY GROUND

"And the children of Israel went into the midst of the sea upon the dry ground: and the waters were a wall unto them on their right hand, and on their left" (Ex. 14:22).

As the Scripture plainly states here, where God opened a path through the Red Sea, the ground was dry. Above that, the water stood like a wall on either side of them, which had to be one of the most astounding sights that man has ever witnessed.

This miracle, which is at least one of the greatest performed in Old Testament times, if not the greatest, is astounding in every respect. It defies several laws, as would be overly obvious, but, of course, God, who originally made the laws of creation, can override them with even greater laws simply because He is the source of all things.

Exodus 15:8 says, *"The floods stood upright as an heap."*

In Psalms 78:13, it is also said, *"He made the waters to stand as an heap."*

THE MIRACLE-WORKING POWER OF GOD

Every true believer knows and understands that God is a miracle-working God. He created this world by and through the performing of miracles. He sustains the world in the same manner, and He continues to perform miracles even unto this very hour and, in fact, will ever continue to do so. As stated, He was, is, and ever shall be a miracle-working God.

Sometime ago, in writing the commentaries, I was studying the word *miracles*.

The Lord spoke to my heart that day and told me that He not only continues to perform miracles, but actually is doing so on a continuing basis, and even to a far greater degree than we could ever grasp or understand.

Let me explain: Anytime the Lord does something for us, whether we are spiritual enough to understand it or not, He has to perform a miracle, and He is constantly working on our behalf. Whatever He does, whether we understand it or not or see it or not, He is performing miracles. In other words, He has to move people, places, things, and events in a certain way in order to bring things to pass, and at the same time, not violate the free moral agency of any individual. All of this can be constituted as none other than miracles.

The sin of man, even the church, is definitely not in overstating the case, but rather understating the case. In fact, I think it's impossible for one to overstate God. As Stewart Hamblin wrote sometime ago, "It is no secret what God can do."

WE SHOULD EXPECT MIRACLES

The believer should expect miracles, should anticipate miracles, and should, in fact, think of them as an everyday occurrence!

While some miracles are certainly more astounding than others, even as we are studying here about the opening of the Red Sea, nevertheless, anything and everything that God does, I think, can be constituted as a miracle. He alone devised the laws of nature that operate this universe, and He, at His own discretion, can circumvent those laws or even override them.

Now, that's not at all unusual! In fact, as God gives man the knowledge and the ability to understand His laws, man is constantly overriding one law with a greater law.

For instance, the law of gravity is obvious to all; however, the Lord has given man the intelligence to also understand and put into motion the laws of aerodynamics. How in the world can an airplane, with some of them weighing many tons, fly through the air when, in fact, it is far heavier than the air? It does so by the operation of law that's even greater than the law of gravity.

In fact, these things are done constantly, so it should not be a surprise to anyone that God, who devised all these laws, can at any time, according to His own discretion, put into effect a law that will supersede or override other laws He has made.

That's what He did at the Red Sea.

THE STRONG EAST WIND

The Lord simply used the law of aerodynamics as it regarded the strong east wind, which overcame the law of gravity. Both were laws that He had created. In fact, that's the very same way that airplanes fly. A jet engine or a propeller instigates a strong wind, which pushes the airplane, holds it up, and overrides the law of gravity that would bring it down, were it able to do so.

So, why do we doubt God when His miracles are explainable, at least to a certain degree, meaning that, in a sense, man constantly does the same.

We don't think of the flying of an airplane as a miracle, just the law of aerodynamics being applied, which overrides the law of gravity, but again, that's the way God performs His miracles. However, He has total knowledge of all laws for the simple reason, as stated, that He devised them, while man only has a limited amount of knowledge. In fact, most of the knowledge of which I speak did not even begin until the beginning of the 20th century. That is in keeping with Daniel's prophecy, given about 2,600 years ago, which said, *"Shut up the words, and seal the book even to the time of the end: many shall run to and fro, and knowledge shall be increased"* (Dan. 12:4).

This plainly tells us that knowledge would be increased in the last days, which we have seen come to pass before our very eyes. Unbelievers scoff at God and scoff at miracles, not realizing how silly are their objections.

UNBELIEF

Sometime back, I happened to see a television program where three unbelievers were going to debate three believers. I was to find out that the unbelief of the believers was about as bad as the unbelief of the unbelievers.

The unbelievers scoffed at any of the miracles recorded in the Old Testament. Three of the miracles—the opening of the Red Sea, the walls of Jericho falling down, and the burn taken out of the fire for the Hebrew children—were to be inspected closely.

Of course, the unbelievers denied the actual happenings of these events, but, as stated, these so-called believers were not so far behind the rank unbelievers.

They tried to explain these miracles by natural phenomena. In other words, they said that an earthquake opened the Red Sea, and, as well, it was an earthquake that destroyed the walls of Jericho. To explain the fiery furnace, they claimed that there is a "cool spot" in the midst of every fire, and the three Hebrew children found this cool spot, and that's the way they survived.

IF ONE CAN EXPLAIN A MIRACLE,
IT'S NOT A MIRACLE

As I listened to this foolishness, and foolishness it was, I wondered why the preachers who claimed to believe in God couldn't just simply say that God did it, and inasmuch as God did it, He was not limited to the ways that He could do it.

The Bible doesn't say there was an earthquake at the time of the opening of the Red Sea, but it does say that God *"caused the sea to go back by a strong east wind all that night, and made the sea dry land, and the waters were divided."*

So, let's quit trying to explain away the miracles of God and just simply understand that God is able to do all things and, in fact, will do all things for those who will believe Him. In other words, I believe in miracles. I think the preachers of my illustration little believe in miracles, if at all. They claim to believe the Bible, but if the truth be known, the Bible that they claim to believe is a very abbreviated Bible, for if you take the miracles out of the Bible, there isn't a whole lot left.

Incidentally, if it was an earthquake that opened the Red Sea and tumbled the Jericho walls, who timed those earthquakes perfectly at the exact time they were needed?

THE EGYPTIANS

"And the Egyptians pursued, and went in after them to the midst of the sea, even all Pharaoh's horses, his chariots, and his horsemen" (Ex. 14:23).

Whether Pharaoh actually went into the Red Sea himself, the Scripture doesn't say. Some scholars believe that he did, and some believe that he didn't.

Exodus 14:10 does say, *"And when Pharaoh drew near,"* insinuating somewhat that Pharaoh may definitely have been with this pursuing army.

Due to all the things that had happened in the intervening months, I choose to believe that the pride of Pharaoh demanded that he lead this charge in this attack, but whether he did or not is not really the point.

WHAT THE RED SEA CROSSING ACTUALLY MEANT

Typically (the type), the crossing of the Red Sea speaks of Christ making a way of redemption by and through the death that He died on the Cross, which He did for all who will believe.

The Red Sea is the figure of death, actually, the boundary line of Satan's power.

Note the words of God to Moses: *"You lift up your rod, and stretch out your hand over the sea, and divide it; and the children of Israel shall go on dry ground through the midst of the sea."*

Moses is plainly a type of Christ and the rod a symbol of His power and authority. The Red Sea completely destroyed the power of Pharaoh (Satan) over God's people.

Hebrews 2:14 gives us the antitype, or how the Lord did this: *"That through death He* (Jesus) *might destroy him who had the power of death, that is, the Devil."*

Some have tried to portray the crossing of the Red Sea as a type of physical death but with it having no power over the child of God, with him going to be with Christ. That's not what this is speaking about.

The opening of the Red Sea, the crossing by the children of Israel, and the defeat of Pharaoh as the waters closed over his army are pictures of what Jesus did for us at the Cross and our death that we died in Him, which Paul explained by saying that we *"were baptized into His death"* (Rom. 6:3).

The children of Israel died to the old life, which was symbolized by the crossing of the Red Sea, and they gained newness of life by being released from the clutches of Pharaoh, who was a type of the Devil.

So, the believer can look at this account given in the Bible and can get a picture of the born-again experience, which brings one from spiritual death to spiritual life.

It was the Cross alone where Satan was totally and completely defeated, even as Pharaoh was completely defeated by the Passover, which typified the death of Christ, and the Red Sea, which typified our part in that death (Col. 2:10-15).

THE PILLAR OF FIRE AND OF THE CLOUD

"And it came to pass, that in the morning watch the LORD looked unto the host of the Egyptians through the pillar of fire and of the cloud, and troubled the host of the Egyptians" (Ex. 14:24).

I think the words "the morning watch" portray to us the fact that the children of Israel began to go into the path formed in the Red Sea immediately that night whenever it began to open. The morning watch of the Hebrews at this period of history lasted from 2 A.M. until sunrise.

Sunrise in Egypt, which would have been early April, would take place at about 6 A.M.

So, the children of Israel were probably about halfway across the body of water—actually walking on dry ground, with a wall of water on either side—when the Egyptians started down after them.

When the Scripture says that the Lord *"troubled the host of the Egyptians"* as they pursued the children of Israel, Josephus further says: "Showers of rain came down from the sky, and dreadful thunders and lightning, with flashes of fire; thunderbolts also were darted upon them; nor was there anything, which could be sent by God upon man as indications of His wrath, which did not happen upon this occasion."

The words *"troubled the host"* in the Hebrew actually mean *"threw it into confusion."*

THE DOCTRINE

Continuing to look at this crossing as it regards it being a type of our salvation in Christ, doctrinally, the passage through the Red Sea sets forth the believers union with Christ in His death and resurrection.

As we've already stated, the Passover proclaimed what Christ did for us, while the Red Sea crossing portrayed our union with Christ as it regards being baptized into His death.

Paul said, *"I am crucified with Christ"* (Gal. 2:20). This refers to our judicial identification with our substitute. That Israel passed through the Red Sea and emerged safely on the far side, as stated, tells of our union with Christ in His death and, as well, tells of the resurrection, our being raised with Him *"in newness of life."*

Paul said, *"If we have been planted together in the likeness of His death, we shall be also in the likeness of His resurrection"* (Rom. 6:5).

He also said, *"When we were dead in sins, has quickened us* (made us spiritually alive) *together with Christ ... And has raised us up together"* (Eph. 2:5-6).

THE LORD FIGHTS FOR US

"And took off their chariot wheels, that they drove them heavily: so that the Egyptians said, Let us flee from the face of Israel; for the LORD *fights for them against the Egyptians"* (Ex. 14:25).

The idea of this passage is that the Lord made useless the chariots of the Egyptians, on which they were so heavily depending.

The Lord evidently so situated the passage that sinkholes appeared, with the chariot wheels bogging up to the axles in those holes, which, in effect, stopped them.

By joining that with lightning bolts darting among them, slashing rain, and perhaps other phenomena, as well—if, in fact, those things actually happened, which they, no doubt, did—it caused the Egyptians to realize that they had just raced into a trap. They saw that the Lord was not only fighting for the children of Israel but was at the same time fighting against the Egyptians.

Let the modern believer understand that we serve the same God served by the children of Israel. As well, He will do the same for us that He did for them. We must understand that and believe that, even as we know that.

THE LORD OVERTHREW THE EGYPTIANS

"And the Lord *said unto Moses, Stretch out your hand over the sea, that the waters may come again upon the Egyptians, upon their chariots, and upon their horsemen. And Moses stretched forth his hand over the sea, and the sea returned to his strength when the morning appeared; and the Egyptians fled against it; and the* Lord *overthrew the Egyptians in the midst of the sea"* (Ex. 14:26-27).

The Lord not only delivered Israel but, as well, defeated the Egyptians. At Cavalry, the Lord not only delivered us, but He also defeated Satan (Col. 2:14-15).

As every Egyptian was totally and completely defeated, Satan was totally and completely defeated, as well, at the Cross. Not one single bondage of darkness was excluded, but rather Jesus addressed them all.

The children of Israel had all safely crossed as a result of the great miracle carried out by the Lord. With all safely on the other side and the mighty army of Egypt bogged down in the very midst of the sea, and now even trying to turn and escape the dark waters, *"the* Lord *said unto Moses, Stretch out your hand over the sea, that the waters may come again upon the Egyptians,"* which he did, and it did.

A wall of water on both sides came crashing down upon this mighty army, and they were as helpless as helplessness could ever be. Exactly as the Lord had said, Israel would see those Egyptians no more.

It should be noticed that God used Moses to open the sea and to close it. Moses was a type of Christ, even as the rod was a type of the Word of God.

The psalmist said, *"Yea, though I walk through the valley of the shadow of death, I will fear no evil: for You are with me; Your rod and Your staff they comfort me"* (Ps. 23:4).

VICTORY

"And the waters returned, and covered the chariots, and the horsemen, and all the host of Pharaoh that came into the sea after them; there remained not so much as one of them. But the children of Israel walked upon dry land in the midst of the sea; and the waters were a wall unto them on their right hand, and on their left" (Ex. 14:28-29).

We as human beings need many things; however, God needs nothing in order to carry out that which He so desires. The elements are at His beck and call. Along with that, if a heart is stubborn and obstinate toward Him, which that is certainly not the way that He would desire it to be, still, He can even use that for His glory, exactly as He used the stubborn, obstinate heart of Pharaoh.

Pharaoh wanted to do what he did, so the Lord allowed

him free rein. It would result in God getting honor and glory and Pharaoh being destroyed, exactly as such incidents have taken place countless times since.

GOD'S WILL

At this very moment, Satan is preparing for the debut of the Antichrist, which will be his trump card of the ages.

However, the Lord will use all of this as an occasion to bring Israel back to Himself, which means that the Devil's plans will, in a sense, be made to work for the Lord, as everything sooner or later is made to work for the Lord. If we are in the center of God's will, then *"we know that all things work together for good to them who love God, to them who are the called according to His purpose"* (Rom. 8:28).

Two things are predicated on *"all things working together for good"* regarding us:
1. We must *"love God."*
2. We must function *"according to His purpose"* and not according to ours. That's what I meant by being in the center of God's will.

It was the will of God for Israel to be delivered, and it is the will of God for you to be delivered. If you'll believe God, stand upon His promises, and look to the Cross where the price was paid—which the deliverance of the children of Israel was but a type—as they were delivered, you will be delivered. It doesn't matter what type of deliverance is needed, God is able!

THE GREAT WORK OF THE LORD

"Thus the LORD saved Israel that day out of the hand of the Egyptians; and Israel saw the Egyptians dead upon the seashore. And Israel saw that great work which the LORD did upon the Egyptians: and the people feared the LORD, and believed the LORD, and His servant Moses" (Ex. 14:30-31).

Evidently a west wind set in, which was assisted by the current, and drove the bodies of the drowned Egyptians to the eastern side of the gulf, where many of them were cast upon the shore.

In this way, according to Josephus, Moses obtained weapons and armor for a considerable number of Israelites. This means that the Egyptians' dead were cast upon the same shore where Israel had come out. It would not have been possible for Israel to have looked over that expanse of water and observe dead bodies on the other shore, which could have been at least 10 or 12 miles away.

The *"great work"* that the Lord performed that day was the destruction of the entire chariot force of Egypt, plus, no doubt, many of her footmen.

In fact, the Egyptian kings mainly relied on their chariot force in times of war.

A GREAT WORK

God always performs a great work. He is still performing

great works, and He shall ever continue to perform great works. I think it can be said without fear of exaggeration or contradiction that, while some may be grander than others, any and every work performed by the Lord could certainly be classed as a great work.

We serve a great God! Therefore, He does great works.

THE RED SEA AND THE JORDAN RIVER

As we close this volume, which portrays one of the greatest miracles ever performed by God, I want us to try to understand the difference between the Red Sea crossing and the Jordan River crossing.

They both have their antitype in the death of Christ, but in the former, we see separation from Egypt, and in the latter, introduction into the land of Canaan.

The idea is this: The Red Sea crossing, as stated, is pictured as our born-again experience as we die to the old life and are made alive to the other.

The Passover typified what Christ has done for us, while the Red Sea crossing typified our being baptized into the death of Christ. This alone guarantees us deliverance from this present evil world and, as well, guarantees us *"newness of life."*

Also, what delivered Israel destroyed the Egyptians, i.e., the Devil.

The Jordan River crossing was very similar, but yet, somewhat different.

If it matters, the Jordan River at the time of the crossing was at flood tide, which means it was about a mile and a half wide and about 40 feet deep. Normally, it's only about 30 to 100 feet in width.

THE INHERITANCE OF THE SAINTS

If it is to be noticed, after Israel had crossed the Jordan, Joshua had them to keep the Passover, which evidently had not been kept in quite some time. This states that the crossing of the Jordan did not specify salvation, as the Red Sea crossing did, with Israel, in fact, already saved.

However, they were commanded to eat the Passover again, even as they were supposed to do on a continuing basis year by year, signifying that just as it had their salvation, their sanctification depended on what Christ did at the Cross. The crossing of the Jordan and the occupation of Canaan did not typify heaven, as some think, but rather our spiritual experience in Christ in the gaining of our inheritance.

So, we find from this, as there had to be a death to Egypt, which typified the world, and which was typified by the Red Sea crossing, likewise, after conversion, there has to be a death to self, typified by the Jordan River crossing, with both crossings being miracles from God. As the sinner cannot save himself, the Christian cannot sanctify himself. Both must be done by the power of the Holy Spirit through the sacrifice of Christ, portraying His shed blood.

"When I see the blood, I will pass over you."

Why did they nail Him to Calvary's tree?
Why? Tell me, why was He there?
Jesus the helper, the healer, the friend,
Why? Tell me, why was He there?

Why should He love me, a sinner undone?
Why? Tell me, why should He care?
I do not merit the love He has shown.
Why? Tell me, why should He care?

Why should I linger afar from His love?
Why? Tell me, why should I fear?
Somehow I know I should venture and prove.
Why? Tell me, why should I fear?

All my iniquities on Him were laid,
He nailed them all to the tree.
Jesus the debt of my sin fully paid,
He paid the ransom for me.

REFERENCES

Introduction

J. Brown, *Expository Discourses on the First Epistle of the Apostle Peter* (R. Carter & Brothers, 1855), 117.

Chapter 1

Arthur W. Pink, *Gleanings in Exodus* (Sovereign Grace Publishers, Lafayette, 2002), 107.

C.H. Mackintosh, *Notes on the Book of Exodus* (New York, Loizeaux Brothers, 1880), 138.

Arthur W. Pink, Gleanings in Exodus (Sovereign Grace Publishers, Lafayette, 2002), 82. Ibid., 88.

Chapter 2

C.H. Mackintosh, *Notes on the Book of Exodus* (New York, Loizeaux Brothers, 1880), 164.

Matthew Henry, *Matthew Henry's Commentary on the Whole Bible* (Hendrickson Publishers, Inc., 1994), Exodus 12:37-42.

Arthur W. Pink, *Gleanings in Exodus* (Sovereign Grace Publishers, Lafayette, 2002), 130.

Chapter 3

C.H. Mackintosh, *Notes on the Book of Exodus* (New York, Loizeaux
Brothers, 1880), 152.

George Williams, *William's Complete Bible Commentary* (Grand Rap-
ids, Kregel Publications, 1994), 50.

Arthur W. Pink, *Gleanings in Exodus* (Sovereign Grace
Publishers, Lafayette, 2002), 134. Ibid., 139.

C.H. Mackintosh, *Notes on the Book of Exodus* (New York, Loizeaux
Brothers, 1880), 171.

Arthur W. Pink, *Gleanings in Exodus* (Sovereign Grace
Publishers, Lafayette, 2002), 142.

C.H. Mackintosh, *Notes on the Book of Exodus* (New York, Loizeaux
Brothers, 1880), 171.

Arthur W. Pink, *Gleanings in Exodus* (Sovereign Grace
Publishers, Lafayette, 2002), 142.

Chapter 4

George Williams, *William's Complete Bible Commentary* (Grand Rap-
ids, Kregel Publications, 1994), 50.

Arthur W. Pink, *Gleanings in Exodus* (Sovereign Grace
Publishers, Lafayette, 2002), 145.

C.H. Mackintosh, *Notes on the Book of Exodus* (New York, Loizeaux
Brothers, 1880), 175.

Matthew Henry, *Matthew Henry's Commentary on the Whole Bible*
(Hendrickson Publishers,Inc., 1994),
Exodus 14:10-14.

Arthur W. Pink, *Gleanings in Exodus* (Sovereign Grace
Publishers, Lafayette, 2002), 109.

C.H. Mackintosh, *Notes on the Book of Exodus* (New York, Loizeaux
Brothers, 1880), 185. Ibid., 188.

ABOUT EVANGELIST JIMMY SWAGGART

The Rev. Jimmy Swaggart is a Pentecostal evangelist whose anointed preaching and teaching has drawn multitudes to the Cross of Christ since 1955.

As an author, he has written more than 50 books, commentaries, study guides, and The Expositor's Study Bible, which has sold more than 2 million copies.

As an award-winning musician and singer, Brother Swaggart has recorded more than 50 gospel albums and sold nearly 16 million recordings worldwide.

For six decades, Brother Swaggart has channeled his preaching and music ministry through multiple media venues including print, radio, television, and the Internet.

In 2010, Jimmy Swaggart Ministries launched its own cable channel, SonLife Broadcasting Network, which airs 24 hours a day to a potential viewing audience of more than 1 billion people around the globe.

Brother Swaggart also pastors Family Worship Center in Baton Rouge, Louisiana, the church home and headquarters of Jimmy Swaggart Ministries.

Jimmy Swaggart Ministries materials can be found at **www.jsm.org**.